Better Homes and Gardens®

Easy EVERYDAY COOKING

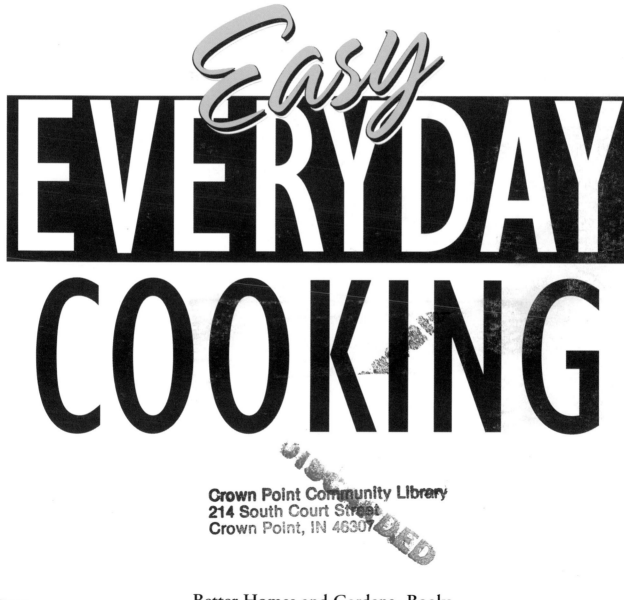

Better Homes and Gardens® Books
Des Moines, Iowa

Our seal assures you that every recipe in *Easy Everyday Cooking* has been tested in the Better Homes and Gardens® Test Kitchen. This means that each recipe is practical and reliable, and meets our high standards of taste appeal. We guarantee your satisfaction with this book for as long as you own it.

Pictured on front cover: Chicken with Peas and Potatoes, page 115

Better Homes and Gardens® Books
An imprint of Meredith® Books

Easy Everyday Cooking
Editor: Carrie Holcomb Mills
Contributing Editor: Spectrum Communication Services, Inc.
Contributing Designers: Seif Visual Communications, Tim Abramowitz
Copy Chief: Terri Fredrickson
Contributing Proofreaders: Gretchen Kauffman, Margaret Smith
Managers, Book Production: Pam Kvitne, Marjorie J. Schenkelberg
Electronic Production Coordinator: Paula Forest
Editorial and Design Assistants: Judy Bailey, Mary Lee Gavin, Karen Schirm
Test Kitchen Director: Lynn Blanchard
Test Kitchen Home Economists: Judy Comstock, Marilyn Cornelius, Jennifer Kalinowski, Maryellyn Krantz, Tami Leonard, Jill Lust, Jill Moberly, Dianna Nolin, Kay Springer, Colleen Weeden, Lori Wilson, Charles Worthington

Meredith® Books
Editor in Chief: James D. Blume
Design Director: Matt Strelecki
Managing Editor: Gregory H. Kayko
Executive Food Editor: Jennifer Dorland Darling

Director, Retail Sales and Marketing: Terry Unsworth
Director, Sales, Special Markets: Rita McMullen
Director, Sales, Premiums: Michael A. Peterson
Director, Sales, Retail: Tom Wierzbicki
Director, Book Marketing: Brad Elmitt
Director, Operations: George A. Susral
Director, Production: Douglas M. Johnston

Vice President, General Manager: Jamie L. Martin

Better Homes and Gardens® Magazine
Editor in Chief: Jean LemMon
Executive Food Editor: Nancy Byal

Meredith Publishing Group
President, Publishing Group: Stephen M. Lacy
Vice President, Finance and Administration: Max Runciman

Meredith Corporation
Chairman and Chief Executive Officer: William T. Kerr

Chairman of the Executive Committee: E. T. Meredith III

DELICIOUS IDEAS FOR NO-FUSS MEALS!

Easy Everyday Cooking offers satisfying solutions for everyday meal preparation. Filled with more than 190 family-pleasing recipes, this appealing collection includes innovative ways to prepare meats, poultry, and seafood as well as ideas for appetizers, soups, salads, vegetarian dishes, and desserts. Choose from tempters such as Herb-Pepper Sirloin Steak, Ruby-Glazed Chicken Breasts, Four Bean Enchiladas, Apple-Blueberry Pastries, Chocolate Cream Cake, and more.

Don't waste a minute. Try some of these exceptional everyday dishes. They're perfect any time and every time.

Contents

Appetizers & SNACKS

Contents

POTTED PEPPER DIP
(recipe, page 8)

Summer Fruit Salsa

The refreshing ingredients in this summer salsa pair well with grilled chicken breasts and fish steaks.

1 tablespoon lime juice 1 tablespoon plum or peach jam ½ cup finely chopped peach ½ cup chopped strawberries ½ cup finely chopped fresh pineapple ½ cup finely chopped plums 2 tablespoons finely chopped red onion 1 jalapeño pepper, seeded and finely chopped Dash ground cloves Jalapeño peppers, cut into thin strips (optional) Baked tortilla chips	In a medium bowl stir together lime juice and plum or peach jam until smooth. Stir in peach, strawberries, pineapple, plums, red onion, finely chopped jalapeño pepper, and cloves. Cover and chill up to 2 hours to blend flavors. If desired, garnish with jalapeño pepper strips. Serve with baked tortilla chips. Makes 8 servings. *Nutrition information per serving: 114 calories, 2 g protein, 21 g carbohydrate, 2 g fat (0 g saturated), 0 mg cholesterol, 120 mg sodium.*

Apples with Cinnamon-Cider Dip

Once cut, the apple slices brown quickly. Sprinkle with lemon or orange juice mixed with a little water, or treat them with an ascorbic acid color keeper.

2 tablespoons cornstarch 1 tablespoon brown sugar 1¼ cups apple cider 3 tablespoons honey 2 teaspoons lemon juice ½ teaspoon ground cinnamon ⅛ teaspoon salt (optional) Dash ground cloves Dash ground allspice 1 tablespoon butter or margarine 4 apples, cored and sliced	For dip, in a medium saucepan combine cornstarch and brown sugar. Stir in apple cider, honey, lemon juice, cinnamon, salt (if desired), cloves, and allspice. Cook and stir until thickened and bubbly. Cook and stir for 2 minutes more. Remove from heat. Add butter or margarine, stirring until melted. Serve dip warm with sliced apples. Makes 4 to 6 servings. *Nutrition information per serving: 221 calories, 0 g protein, 51 g carbohydrate, 3 g fat (2 g saturated), 8 mg cholesterol, 34 mg sodium.*

Apples with Cinnamon-Cider Dip

Potted Pepper Dip

For an eye-catching presentation, use an assortment of colorful sweet peppers. If you want to make a lower-fat dip, use fat-free cream cheese and fat-free mayonnaise or salad dressing in place of the regular products.

2 tablespoons lemon juice
2 teaspoons olive oil or cooking oil
1 teaspoon sugar
¼ teaspoon salt
Dash black pepper
1 small onion, cut up
4 large red, green, yellow, or orange
   sweet peppers, seeded and cut up*
1 8-ounce package cream cheese,
   softened
¼ cup mayonnaise or salad dressing
1 teaspoon prepared horseradish
Few dashes bottled hot pepper sauce
2 or 3 red, yellow, and/or orange
   sweet peppers, tops removed and
   seeded
Assorted vegetable dippers and/or
   breadsticks
Fresh herbs (optional)

In a blender container or food processor bowl combine the lemon juice, oil, sugar, salt, and black pepper. Add the onion and about one-third of the cut-up sweet peppers.

Cover and blend or process until smooth. Add the remaining cut-up sweet peppers. Cover and blend or process until smooth. Transfer the mixture to a medium bowl. Cover and let stand at room temperature at least 2 hours.

Place pureed vegetable mixture in a sieve and press gently to drain off excess liquid. In a medium bowl combine cream cheese, mayonnaise or salad dressing, horseradish, and hot pepper sauce. Stir in the pureed vegetable mixture. Cover and chill for 2 to 3 hours.

Spoon into the whole sweet pepper shells. Place filled peppers in the center of a serving platter; surround with vegetable dippers and/or breadsticks. If desired, garnish with fresh herbs. Makes about 2 cups.

*Note: To avoid getting tough pepper skins in the dip, cook seeded, quartered sweet peppers in boiling water for a few seconds. When cool enough to handle, peel off skins with a small knife and cut peppers into pieces.

Nutrition information per tablespoon dip: 46 calories, 1 g protein, 2 g carbohydrate, 4 g fat (2 g saturated), 9 mg cholesterol, 50 mg sodium.

Creamy Onion Dip

We pepped up this version of a popular dip with a little crumbled blue cheese.

1½ cups dairy sour cream
2 tablespoons dry onion soup mix
½ cup crumbed blue cheese (2 ounces)
Snipped parsley (optional)
Assorted vegetable dippers (such as carrot, zucchini, jicama, or red sweet pepper strips, and/or broccoli or cauliflower flowerets)

In a medium mixing bowl stir together the sour cream and dry onion soup mix. Stir in blue cheese. Cover and chill up to 48 hours.

If desired, sprinkle with snipped parsley. Serve with vegetable dippers. Makes about 1¾ cups.

Nutrition information per tablespoon dip: 37 calories, 1 g protein, 1 g carbohydrate, 3 g fat (2 g saturated), 7 mg cholesterol, 103 mg sodium.

Monterey Jack Fondue

Monterey Jack cheese could be called the American mozzarella. Long known in California, it became available across the nation in the late '60s. It's great shredded over Mexican foods, such as enchiladas, or used in a grilled cheese sandwich.

3 tablespoons margarine or butter
3 tablespoons all-purpose flour
1 teaspoon dried minced onion
⅛ teaspoon garlic powder
⅛ teaspoon ground red pepper
1 5-ounce can (⅔ cup) evaporated milk
½ cup chicken broth
1¼ cups shredded Monterey Jack cheese (5 ounces)
French bread cubes

In a small saucepan melt margarine or butter. Stir in flour, dried minced onion, garlic powder, and red pepper. Stir in milk and chicken broth all at once.

Cook and stir until thickened and bubbly. Gradually add Monterey Jack cheese, stirring until cheese is melted. Transfer to a fondue pot; place over fondue burner.

Serve the fondue with bread cubes. (Add additional chicken broth, as necessary, for desired consistency.) Makes 6 servings.

Nutrition information per serving: 249 calories, 9 g protein, 18 g carbohydrate, 16 g fat (7 g saturated), 28 mg cholesterol, 418 mg sodium.

Baked Kasseri Cheese Spread

When chilly winds blow, cozy up to the fire and linger over a glass of red wine, a loaf of crusty bread, and this creamy spread of kasseri cheese, piquant olives, and oregano.

12   ounces kasseri or Scamorza cheese
⅔   cup kalamata olives, pitted and
        quartered
2   tablespoons snipped fresh oregano
1   clove garlic, minced
¼   teaspoon crushed red pepper
        French bread slices, apple slices, or
        assorted crackers

Cut kasseri or Scamorza cheese into ½-inch slices. Layer cheese in the bottom of a shallow 1-quart quiche dish or a 9-inch pie plate, overlapping if necessary. Toss together the olives, oregano, garlic, and red pepper. Sprinkle over the cheese.

Bake in a 450° oven for 8 to 10 minutes or until cheese just starts to melt. Serve immediately on bread, apple slices, or assorted crackers. Rewarm cheese as needed. Makes 12 servings.

Nutrition information per serving (spread only): 141 calories, 7 g protein, 1 g carbohydrate, 12 g fat (7 g saturated), 30 mg cholesterol, 350 mg sodium.

Smoky Cheese Ball

We found the distinct flavor of smoked cheddar enticing, but you can use regular cheddar if you prefer.

2   8-ounce packages cream cheese
2   cups shredded smoky cheddar
        cheese (8 ounces)
½   cup margarine or butter
2   tablespoons milk
2   teaspoons steak sauce
¾   cup finely chopped almonds or
        pecans, toasted

Bring cream cheese, cheddar cheese, and margarine or butter to room temperature. In a large mixing bowl combine the cream cheese, cheddar cheese, margarine or butter, milk, and steak sauce.

Beat cheese mixture on medium speed of an electric mixer until fluffy. Cover and chill for 30 minutes. Shape cheese mixture into a ball. Roll in almonds or pecans to coat, patting nuts onto ball to secure. Makes 1 large ball (5 cups).

Nutrition information per tablespoon spread: 45 calories, 1 g protein, 0 g carbohydrate, 4 g fat (3 g saturated), 12 mg cholesterol, 49 mg sodium.

Baked Kasseri Cheese Spread

Deviled Peanuts

These spicy peanuts or pumpkin seeds make a perfect snack to serve with a before-dinner drink such as sparkling water, hot-style tomato juice, or Mexican beer.

2	tablespoons margarine or butter
1	tablespoon lime juice or lemon juice
1	teaspoon ground cumin
1	teaspoon black pepper
½	to 1 teaspoon ground red pepper
¼	teaspoon salt
3	cups raw peanuts or shelled raw pumpkin seeds (1 pound)

In a saucepan combine margarine or butter, lime juice or lemon juice, cumin, black pepper, ground red pepper, and salt. Cook and stir until margarine is melted. Stir in the peanuts or shelled pumpkin seeds. Toss lightly to coat.

Spread the peanuts or pumpkin seeds in a 13x9x2-inch baking pan. Bake in a 350° oven for 15 to 20 minutes or until toasted, stirring occasionally. Cool before serving. Makes 24 servings.

Nutrition information per serving: 114 calories, 5 g protein, 3 g carbohydrate, 10 g fat (2 g saturated), 0 mg cholesterol, 38 mg sodium.

Curried Snack Mix

Do you crave salty, high-fat snacks, such as potato chips? Bake a batch of this snack mix and you'll save yourself about half the calories and more than half the fat of a similar serving of fat-laden chips.

3	plain rice cakes, broken into bite-size pieces
1	cup bite-size corn square cereal or oyster crackers
¾	cup pretzel sticks, halved (1 ounce)
1	tablespoon margarine or butter, melted
1	teaspoon Worcestershire sauce
½	to ¾ teaspoon curry powder

In a 13x9x2-inch baking pan stir together broken rice cakes, corn cereal or oyster crackers, and pretzels. In a custard cup stir together melted margarine or butter, Worcestershire sauce, and curry powder.

Drizzle curry mixture over cereal mixture. Toss gently to coat. Bake in a 300° oven for 20 minutes, stirring twice. Cool before serving. Store leftovers in a tightly covered container. Makes 6 to 8 servings.

Nutrition information per serving: 76 calories, 1 g protein, 12 g carbohydrate, 2 g fat (1 g saturated), 0 mg cholesterol, 175 mg sodium.

Curried Snack Mix

Sugar and Spice Popcorn

Why eat plain popcorn when you can enjoy this version spiced with cinnamon, nutmeg, and ginger?

Nonstick spray coating
6 cups popped popcorn (using no oil)
2 tablespoons sugar
2 teaspoons water
¼ teaspoon ground cinnamon
⅛ teaspoon ground nutmeg
⅛ teaspoon ground ginger

Spray a 13x9x2-inch baking pan with nonstick coating. Place the popcorn in the pan.

In a small bowl stir together sugar, water, cinnamon, nutmeg, and ginger. Drizzle the spice mixture over popcorn. Toss gently to coat. Bake in a 350° oven for 15 minutes, stirring once or twice.

Transfer the hot popcorn to a large piece of foil. Cool completely. Store leftovers in a tightly covered container. Makes 8 servings.

Nutrition information per serving: 32 calories, 1 g protein, 7 g carbohydrate, 0 g fat (0 g saturated), 0 mg cholesterol, 0 mg sodium.

Nachos de Mer

If the Scandinavians had invented nachos, they might taste something like this. Reminiscent of the northlanders' famed open-faced sandwiches, toasted pita wedges are topped with a delicate seafood salad.

Toasted Pita Wedges
1 cup finely chopped, seeded plum tomatoes
⅓ cup finely chopped red or green sweet pepper
1½ cups chopped cooked shrimp or crabmeat
2 tablespoons mayonnaise or salad dressing
1 tablespoon finely chopped green onion
2 teaspoons Dijon-style mustard
1½ teaspoons snipped fresh dill
⅛ teaspoon salt
1½ cups shredded Havarti or Swiss cheese (6 ounces)

Prepare Toasted Pita Wedges. Set aside. In a small bowl combine tomatoes and sweet pepper. In a medium bowl combine shrimp or crabmeat, mayonnaise or salad dressing, green onion, mustard, dill, and salt. Stir in shredded cheese. If desired, cover and chill both mixtures up to 4 hours.

Place the pita wedges on 2 large baking sheets. Top with shrimp mixture. Bake in a 350° oven for 5 to 6 minutes or until cheese starts to melt. Top with tomato mixture. Serve warm. Makes 18 servings.

Toasted Pita Wedges: Split 3 *pita bread rounds* in half horizontally. Cut each circle into 6 wedges. Place the wedges in a single layer on 2 large baking sheets. Bake in a 350° oven for 8 to 10 minutes or until wedges just start to brown. If desired, seal cooled wedges in a plastic bag and store overnight at room temperature. Makes 36 wedges.

Nutrition information per serving: 91 calories, 6 g protein, 7 g carbohydrate, 4 g fat (2 g saturated), 34 mg cholesterol, 145 mg sodium.

HELP YOURSELF TO HAVARTI

When you're looking for an appetizer cheese to serve with wine or to use in recipes such as Nachos de Mer (above), Havarti (ha-VART-ee) is hard to beat. This cream-colored cheese has a porous texture with small irregular holes and varies in flavor from mild to pungent. Besides making great appetizers, Havarti also is delicious in sandwiches or as a dessert with fruit.

Ratatouille Pizza

A ready-made Italian bread shell makes pizza preparation ever so easy. This garden-fresh version takes four different vegetables, arranges them on top of a tongue-tingling tomato sauce, and sprinkles the entire concoction with feta and mozzarella cheeses.

1   small eggplant (12 ounces)
2   tablespoons olive oil or cooking oil
½   cup chopped onion
2   cloves garlic, minced
4   medium tomatoes, peeled, seeded, and chopped (about 2⅔ cups)
1   tablespoon snipped fresh oregano or thyme, or 1 teaspoon dried oregano or thyme, crushed
½   teaspoon sugar
¼   teaspoon salt
⅛   teaspoon pepper
1   12-inch Italian bread shell (Boboli)
2   medium red and/or yellow tomatoes, halved lengthwise and thinly sliced
1   small zucchini, thinly sliced
1   small yellow summer squash, thinly sliced
⅓   cup crumbled feta cheese
2   tablespoons sliced pitted ripe olives
½   cup shredded mozzarella cheese (2 ounces)
    Small fresh oregano or thyme leaves (optional)

Chop enough of the eggplant to make 1 cup. Halve the remaining eggplant lengthwise and thinly slice.

In a medium skillet heat 1 tablespoon of the oil. Add onion and garlic and cook until onion is tender. Stir in chopped eggplant, chopped tomatoes, snipped fresh or dried oregano or thyme, sugar, salt, and pepper. Cook, uncovered, over medium-low heat about 15 minutes or until liquid is evaporated and mixture is of spreading consistency, stirring occasionally during cooking. Remove from heat.

Place the bread shell on a lightly greased baking sheet. Spread the warm tomato mixture over bread shell. Arrange the eggplant and tomato slices around the outside edge of the bread shell. Arrange zucchini and yellow squash slices in the center. Brush vegetables with the remaining oil. Sprinkle with feta cheese and olives. Top with mozzarella cheese.

Bake in a 400° oven for 12 to 15 minutes or until the vegetables are warm and cheese is melted. Transfer to a serving platter. If desired, garnish with fresh oregano or thyme leaves. Cut into wedges. Makes 12 servings.

Nutrition information per serving: 180 calories, 8 g protein, 23 g carbohydrate, 7 g fat (2 g saturated), 11 mg cholesterol, 366 mg sodium.

Crostini

These crisp slices of French bread are topped with a piquant tomato, olive, and chile pepper mixture. Be sure to drain the topping well to prevent the bread from becoming soggy.

2 medium ripe tomatoes, peeled, seeded, and chopped (1 cup)
4 kalamata olives, pitted and chopped, or pitted ripe olives, chopped
¼ cup finely chopped red onion
1 canned anchovy fillet, drained, patted dry, and chopped (optional)
1 tablespoon finely chopped poblano chile pepper
1 tablespoon balsamic vinegar or red wine vinegar
1 large clove garlic, minced
1 8-ounce loaf baguette-style French bread
5 ounces mozzarella cheese, thinly sliced

In a medium bowl stir together tomatoes, olives, red onion, anchovy (if desired), poblano chile pepper, vinegar, and garlic. Let stand at room temperature for 20 to 30 minutes.

Meanwhile, bias-slice bread into ½-inch slices. Place bread slices on a baking sheet. Bake in a 350° oven about 5 minutes or until light brown. Turn bread over and bake for 5 minutes more.

Arrange mozzarella cheese slices on toasted bread. Drain tomato mixture. Top bread slices with the tomato mixture. Bake about 5 minutes more or until cheese is melted and tomato mixture is heated through. Makes about 20 crostini.

Nutrition information per crostini: 54 calories, 3 g protein, 7 g carbohydrate, 2 g fat (1 g saturated), 4 mg cholesterol, 114 mg sodium.

KEEPING HOT FOODS HOT

How to keep hot appetizers warm is a problem party givers always try to solve. The answer doesn't require a maid or a magician—just heat one round of appetizers at a time. This way, another batch will be coming out of the oven just as the last batch is eaten. Or, if you own an electric skillet, hot tray, griddle, or bun warmer, use one of these appliances to keep cooked appetizers hot.

Quesadillas

American-made Mexican cheeses are now available in supermarkets. Look for asadero, Chihuahua, or queso quesadilla for their superior melting qualities.

1 medium Anaheim chile pepper or one 4-ounce can diced green chile peppers, drained

1½ cups shredded asadero, Chihuahua, queso quesadilla, or Monterey Jack cheese (6 ounces)

6 8-inch flour tortillas

1 cup shredded cooked chicken

½ cup chopped seeded tomato (1 small)

3 tablespoons finely chopped green onions

1 tablespoon snipped cilantro, fresh oregano, or basil

Guacamole (optional)

Salsa (optional)

Cilantro leaves (optional)

If using the Anaheim chile pepper, halve pepper lengthwise; remove seeds and membrane. Cut pepper halves into thin slivers.

Sprinkle ¼ cup of the shredded cheese over half of each tortilla. Sprinkle pepper slivers or canned green chile peppers, chicken, tomato, green onions, and snipped cilantro, oregano, or basil over cheese. Fold tortillas in half, pressing gently.

In a large skillet or on a griddle cook quesadillas, 2 at a time, over medium heat for 3 to 4 minutes or until lightly browned, turning once. Remove quesadillas from skillet and place on a baking sheet. Keep warm in a 300° oven. Repeat with remaining quesadillas.

To serve, cut quesadillas in half. If desired, serve with Guacamole and salsa and garnish with cilantro leaves. Makes 12 servings.

Guacamole: In a medium bowl mash 2 medium ripe *avocados,* seeded and peeled, with 1 tablespoon *lemon juice* (mixture will be lumpy). In a food processor bowl or blender container combine 1 small chopped seeded *tomato;* ½ cup chopped *onion;* 2 tablespoons snipped *cilantro;* and 1 or 2 *serrano* or *jalapeño peppers,* seeded and finely chopped. Cover and process or blend until finely chopped. Stir tomato mixture and ¼ teaspoon *salt* into mashed avocado. Transfer to a serving bowl. Makes about 2½ cups.

Nutrition information per serving: 124 calories, 9 g protein, 11 g carbohydrate, 5 g fat (2 g saturated), 24 mg cholesterol, 238 mg sodium.

Fruited Cheese Spirals

Finger food gets a fresh new look! Dried fruit adds jewel tones to these clever spirals filled with prosciutto, cream cheese, and the cinnamon-pepper flavor of fresh basil.

½ cup orange juice or apple juice
1 cup dried fruit (such as cranberries, snipped tart or sweet cherries, and/or snipped apricots)
1 8-ounce tub cream cheese
½ cup dairy sour cream or plain yogurt
¼ cup fresh basil leaves, finely snipped
2 14- to 15-inch soft cracker bread rounds or four 7- to 8-inch flour tortillas
4 very thin slices prosciutto or fully cooked ham
   Fresh basil leaves (optional)
   Orange slices (optional)

In a small saucepan bring the orange juice or apple juice to boiling. Stir in dried fruit; remove from heat. Cover and let stand about 15 minutes or until fruit is softened. Drain. Meanwhile, in a medium mixing bowl stir together cream cheese, sour cream or yogurt, and the ¼ cup finely snipped basil.

Spread cream cheese mixture evenly over one side of each cracker bread or tortilla. Sprinkle each with the softened fruit. Place some of the prosciutto or ham near an edge of each round. Starting from the edge closest to meat, tightly roll up. Wrap each roll in plastic wrap and chill for 4 to 24 hours.

To serve, cut each roll into 1-inch slices. If desired, garnish with additional basil leaves and orange slices. Makes about 24 servings.

Nutrition information per serving: 115 calories, 3 g protein, 14 g carbohydrate, 6 g fat (2 g saturated), 12 mg cholesterol, 142 mg sodium.

*A*PPETIZER PARTY HINTS

When you plan an appetizer party, imagine how foods will look and taste together. Balance rich, highly flavored foods with simple, fresh ones. Plan one or two hot appetizers that can be made ahead and heated just before serving. Also select several chilled appetizers that can be prepared early and served without last-minute attention. If you serve buffet style, choose foods that guests can pick up easily. Too many choices that must be spooned out, sliced, or spread may cause people to bunch around the buffet table.

Jamaican Shrimp

Jamaican cooks usually use Scotch bonnet peppers instead of jalapeño peppers in their spicy dishes. Scotch bonnets, one of the hottest of the chile peppers, add fire to this recipe. Use them if they're available and you like your shrimp hot, hot, hot.

2 pounds fresh or frozen large shrimp in shells
¼ cup salad oil
3 tablespoons white wine vinegar
2 tablespoons lime juice
1 jalapeño pepper, seeded and finely chopped
1 tablespoon honey
2 teaspoons Jamaican Jerk Seasoning
Leaf lettuce (optional)
1 medium mango, peeled, pitted, sliced, and halved crosswise
1 small lime, halved lengthwise and sliced
1 small red onion, quartered and thinly sliced

Rinse shrimp. In a large saucepan cook the fresh or frozen shrimp in boiling, lightly salted water for 1 to 3 minutes or until shrimp turn pink. Drain immediately and cool. Peel and devein shrimp, leaving tails intact. Place shrimp in a plastic bag and set the bag into a shallow dish. (At this point, you can seal the bag and chill up to 24 hours.)

For marinade, in a screw-top jar combine oil, white wine vinegar, lime juice, jalapeño pepper, honey, and Jamaican Jerk Seasoning. Cover and shake well. Pour over the shrimp; seal bag. Marinate in the refrigerator for 1 hour, turning bag occasionally.

Drain shrimp, reserving marinade. If desired, line a large platter with lettuce. Arrange the shrimp, mango, lime, and red onion on top of lettuce. Drizzle with the marinade. Makes 10 to 12 servings.

Jamaican Jerk Seasoning: In a small mixing bowl combine 2 teaspoons *onion powder,* 1 teaspoon *sugar,* 1 teaspoon *salt,* 1 teaspoon ground *thyme,* ½ teaspoon ground *allspice,* ¼ teaspoon ground *cinnamon,* and ¼ teaspoon ground *red pepper.*

Nutrition information per serving: 128 calories, 11 g protein, 7 g carbohydrate, 6 g fat (1 g saturated), 105 mg cholesterol, 174 mg sodium.

Frosty Fruit Smoothie

Here's a kid-pleasing snack that's especially rich in vitamin C.

1 medium banana, peeled and cut into chunks 1 cup orange, pineapple, grape, or apple juice or low-calorie cranberry juice, chilled ½ cup fat-free milk 1 teaspoon vanilla 3 ice cubes	In a blender container combine the banana chunks, chilled fruit juice, milk, vanilla, and ice cubes. Cover and blend until frothy. Pour mixture into glasses. Serve immediately. Makes 2 (10-ounce) servings. *Nutrition information per serving: 137 calories, 4 g protein, 30 g carbohydrate, 1 g fat (0 g saturated), 1 mg cholesterol, 34 mg sodium.*

Apple Sunrise

Make ice cubes from apple or cranberry juice to float in a glass of this refreshing drink.

1 cup apple juice or apple cider, chilled 1 cup low-calorie cranberry juice, chilled ½ cup chilled club soda Ice cubes 2 orange slices (optional)	In a 1-quart measuring cup stir together apple juice or cider, cranberry juice, and club soda. Fill tall glasses with ice cubes. Pour the apple juice mixture over ice. If desired, cut a slit in each orange slice and twist one over the rim of each glass. Makes 2 (10-ounce) servings. *Nutrition information per serving: 85 calories, 0 g protein, 21 g carbohydrate, 0 g fat (0 g saturated), 0 mg cholesterol, 26 mg sodium.*

Iced Espresso

Orange Yogurt Drink

Yogurt, fat-free milk, and fat-free sour cream make this beverage taste positively dreamy.

2½ cups fat-free milk
2 8-ounce cartons vanilla, lemon, or
   orange low-fat yogurt
½ cup fat-free or light dairy sour cream
¼ cup frozen orange or apple juice
   concentrate, thawed

In a pitcher combine milk, yogurt, sour cream, and orange or apple juice concentrate. Beat with a wire whisk or rotary beater until smooth.

Serve immediately or chill. Store leftovers in the refrigerator. Makes 8 (5-ounce) servings.

Nutrition information per serving: 116 calories, 7 g protein, 19 g carbohydrate, 1 g fat (1 g saturated), 5 mg cholesterol, 90 mg sodium.

Iced Espresso

Besides being a refreshing between-meal pick-me-up, this frosty coffee drink is wonderful after a light lunch or dinner in place of dessert.

½ cup ground espresso coffee or
   French roast coffee
1 teaspoon finely shredded orange
   peel
4 cups water
1½ cups fat-free milk
3 tablespoons sugar
   Ice cubes
   Orange peel strips (optional)
1 teaspoon grated semisweet chocolate
   (optional)

Prepare coffee with shredded orange peel and water in a drip coffeemaker or percolator according to the manufacturer's directions. Pour into a heatproof pitcher; stir in milk and sugar. Chill until serving time.

To serve, fill 6 glasses with ice cubes. Pour the coffee mixture over the ice. If desired, garnish each serving with an orange peel strip and grated chocolate. Makes 6 (6-ounce) servings.

Nutrition information per serving: 54 calories, 2 g protein, 11 g carbohydrate, 0 g fat (0 g saturated), 1 mg cholesterol, 35 mg sodium.

Salads,
SOUPS & STEWS

Contents

SPICY STEAK & RANCH SALAD
recipe, page 32)

Taco Salad

Although a tomatillo (tohm ah TEE oh) looks like a small green tomato, its flavor is a combination of lemon, apple, and herbs. Look for canned tomatillos in the Mexican foods section of your supermarket.

Tortilla Cups
Tomatillo Guacamole
8 ounces lean ground beef
3 cloves garlic, minced
1 15-ounce can dark red kidney beans, rinsed and drained
1 8-ounce jar taco sauce
¾ cup frozen whole kernel corn
1 tablespoon chili powder
8 cups torn leaf lettuce or iceberg lettuce
2 medium tomatoes, chopped
1 large green sweet pepper, chopped
¾ cup shredded sharp cheddar cheese (3 ounces)
4 green onions, thinly sliced

Prepare Tortilla Cups; set aside. Prepare Tomatillo Guacamole; chill.

In a medium skillet cook ground beef and garlic until beef is brown. Drain off fat. Stir in beans, taco sauce, corn, and chili powder. Bring to boiling; reduce heat. Cover and simmer for 10 minutes.

In large bowl combine lettuce, tomatoes, green pepper, cheese, and green onions. Divide the lettuce mixture among the Tortilla Cups. Top each with some of the beef mixture and the Tomatillo Guacamole. Makes 6 servings.

Tortilla Cups: Lightly brush six 9- or 10-inch *flour tortillas* with a small amount of *water* or spray *nonstick spray coating* onto 1 side of each tortilla. Spray nonstick coating into 6 small oven-safe bowls or 16-ounce individual casseroles. Press tortillas, coated sides up, into bowls or casseroles. Place a ball of foil into each tortilla cup. Bake in a 350° oven for 15 to 20 minutes or until light brown. Remove foil; cool. Remove Tortilla Cups from bowls. Serve immediately or store in an airtight container for up to 5 days.

Tomatillo Guacamole: Rinse, drain, and finely chop 4 canned *tomatillos* (about ⅓ cup). In a small mixing bowl combine tomatillos; ½ of a small seeded, peeled, and chopped *avocado* (about ½ cup); 2 tablespoons chopped canned *green chile peppers,* drained; and ⅛ teaspoon *garlic salt.* Cover and chill for up to 24 hours. Makes about ¾ cup.

Nutrition information per serving: 398 calories, 22 g protein, 49 g carbohydrate, 17 g fat (6 g saturated), 38 mg cholesterol, 801 mg sodium.

Spicy Steak & Ranch Salad

Steak and onions as you've never seen them before! Sirloin is perked up by Cajun seasoning before slicing, then arranged on tossed greens and topped with a scattering of crispy French-fried onions. This new version of the classic combo has the makings of an instant favorite.

½ cup French-fried onions
1 tablespoon Cajun seasoning
1 tablespoon lime juice
1 clove garlic, minced
1 pound boneless beef top sirloin
   steak, cut 1 inch thick
   Salt (optional)
1 10-ounce package European-style
   salad greens (iceberg lettuce,
   romaine, radicchio, escarole, and
   endive)
2 carrots, peeled into thin strips or cut
   into thin bite-size strips
½ cup thinly sliced radishes
½ cup bottled fat-free ranch salad
   dressing

In a large nonstick skillet cook French-fried onions over medium-high heat about 2 minutes or until browned, stirring occasionally. Set aside.

Meanwhile, combine Cajun seasoning, lime juice, and garlic; rub over both sides of steak. In the same skillet cook steak over medium heat to desired doneness, turning once. (Allow 6 to 8 minutes for medium rare or 9 to 12 minutes for medium.) Remove skillet from heat; let stand for 10 minutes. Cut steak into thin bite-size slices. If desired, season with salt.

In a large bowl toss together the salad greens, carrots, and radishes. Divide among 4 salad bowls or plates. Arrange steak strips over greens mixture. Drizzle dressing over salads. Sprinkle with onions. Makes 4 servings.

Nutrition information per serving: 310 calories, 28 g protein, 16 g carbohydrate, 13 g fat (4 g saturated fat), 76 mg cholesterol, 557 mg sodium.

Pacific Rim Grilled Pork Salad

This dazzling salad blends grilled pork with ingredients from the cuisines of the eastern rim of the Pacific Ocean—soy sauce, ginger, hoisin sauce, rice wine vinegar, sesame oil, and enoki mushrooms.

⅓ cup water
¼ cup dry sherry
¼ cup soy sauce
4 teaspoons grated gingerroot
3 cloves garlic, minced
1 1½-pound boneless pork loin roast, cut into ½-inch-thick slices
¼ cup hoisin sauce
2 tablespoons brown sugar
2 tablespoons salad oil
2 tablespoons rice wine vinegar or white wine vinegar
1 tablespoon toasted sesame oil
12 cups torn spinach
6 thin red onion slices, separated into rings
1 tablespoon sesame seed, toasted (optional)
1 pound plums, pitted and sliced (3 cups)
Enoki mushrooms (optional)

For marinade, in a small mixing bowl combine water, sherry, soy sauce, gingerroot, and garlic. Reserve 2 tablespoons of the marinade for the dressing. Place meat in a plastic bag set in a large bowl. Pour remaining marinade over meat. Close bag. Marinate in the refrigerator for 1 hour.

Drain meat; discard marinade. Grill meat on uncovered grill directly over medium-hot coals for 10 to 12 minutes or until slightly pink in center, turning once.

Meanwhile, for dressing, in a saucepan combine the reserved marinade, hoisin sauce, brown sugar, salad oil, and rice wine vinegar or white wine vinegar. Bring to boiling. Stir in sesame oil. Remove from heat.

Thinly slice meat into bite-size strips. In a large salad bowl combine meat, spinach, onion slices, and, if desired, sesame seed. Pour hot dressing over meat mixture. Toss gently to coat.

Serve on salad plates with plum slices. If desired, top with enoki mushrooms. Makes 6 servings.

Nutrition information per serving: 310 calories, 21 g protein, 22 g carbohydrate, 16 g fat (4 g saturated), 51 mg cholesterol, 1,159 mg sodium.

Peppered Pork & Apricot Salad

Dazzle guests with a main-dish salad whose vibrant colors—bright green, apricot, and black and cream—make a statement on the serving plates. Use quick-cooking pork tenderloin, then slice it into appealing medallions.

12 ounces pork tenderloin
 1 teaspoon coarsely ground pepper
 1 6-ounce package long-grain and wild rice mix
 ½ cup snipped dried apricots
 ¼ cup fat-free Italian salad dressing
 2 green onions, thinly sliced
 2 tablespoons frozen orange juice concentrate, thawed
 ½ cup frozen peas
   Fresh apricots, pitted and sliced (optional)

Trim fat from meat. Place meat on a rack in a shallow roasting pan. Sprinkle the meat with pepper. Insert a meat thermometer into the center of meat. Roast, uncovered, in a 425° oven for 25 to 35 minutes or until the meat thermometer registers 155°. Remove from oven and cover with foil. Let stand for 10 minutes.

Meanwhile, prepare rice mix according to package directions, adding the dried apricots during the last 5 minutes of cooking. Spread mixture in a shallow baking pan and cool for 20 minutes.

For dressing, in a small bowl combine salad dressing, green onions, and orange juice concentrate. In a large bowl combine rice mixture and peas. Drizzle with dressing. Toss gently to coat. Spoon rice mixture onto salad plates. Cut meat crosswise into thin slices; arrange meat on rice mixture. If desired, garnish with fresh apricots. Makes 4 servings.

Nutrition information per serving: 356 calories, 25 g protein, 50 g carbohydrate, 6 g fat (2 g saturated), 61 mg cholesterol, 1,056 mg sodium.

SNIPPING APRICOTS MADE EASY

To snip dried apricots quickly and easily, place apricot halves in a 1-cup glass measure and use kitchen shears or scissors to snip the fruit. Dipping the shears in cold water between snips will keep the apricot pieces from sticking to the shears.

Greek Salad with Herb Vinaigrette

No leftover lamb around? Broil some lamb chops to medium-rare. Then, chill the chops completely before slicing them into thin strips.

3	cups torn curly endive or romaine
1½	cups torn spinach or iceberg lettuce
6	ounces cooked lean lamb or beef, cut into bite-size strips
1	medium tomato, chopped
½	small cucumber, thinly sliced
6	radishes, sliced
2	tablespoons sliced pitted ripe olives
½	cup crumbled feta cheese (2 ounces)
2	green onions, thinly sliced
½	cup Herb Vinaigrette
3	anchovy fillets, drained, rinsed, and patted dry (optional)

Toss together curly endive or romaine and spinach or lettuce. Divide greens among 3 salad plates.

Arrange meat strips, chopped tomato, sliced cucumber, sliced radishes, and olives on greens. Sprinkle with feta cheese and green onions. Shake Herb Vinaigrette well. Drizzle over salads. If desired, top with anchovy fillets. Makes 3 servings.

Herb Vinaigrette: In a screw-top jar combine ½ cup *salad oil;* ⅓ cup *white wine vinegar* or *vinegar;* 1 tablespoon *sugar;* 2 teaspoons snipped *fresh* or ½ teaspoon crushed *dried thyme, oregano,* or *basil;* ½ teaspoon *paprika;* ¼ teaspoon *dry mustard;* and ⅛ teaspoon *pepper.* Cover and shake well. Store dressing in the refrigerator for up to 2 weeks. Shake well before using. Makes about ¾ cup.

Nutrition information per serving: 431 calories, 20 g protein, 11 g carbohydrate, 35 g fat (8 g saturated), 69 mg cholesterol, 325 mg sodium.

Curly Endive Cues

Also known as chicory, curly endive has crisp, frilly, narrow dark green leaves and a prickly texture. Look for heads with crisp, fresh leaves and no discoloration. Store the endive tightly wrapped in the refrigerator for up to 3 days. To use, rinse well in cold water and pat dry with paper towels.

Grilled California Chicken Salad

For a variation, try this refreshing salad with yellow wax beans instead of green beans and sliced carambola (star fruit) instead of the mango. (Also pictured on the cover.)

Cilantro Vinaigrette
2   medium skinless, boneless chicken
      breast halves (about 8 ounces
      total)
1   cup green beans
4   cups shredded mixed greens
1   orange, sliced
1   mango, seeded, peeled, and sliced
      Chopped peanuts or toasted sesame
        seed (optional)

Prepare the Cilantro Vinaigrette. Reserve half of the vinaigrette for dressing. Rinse chicken; pat dry with paper towels. In a medium bowl combine remaining vinaigrette and chicken. Cover and marinate in the refrigerator for 30 minutes. Drain, reserving marinade.

Grill chicken on an uncovered grill directly over medium coals for 9 minutes. Turn chicken and brush with reserved marinade; grill 3 to 6 minutes more or until tender and no longer pink. Discard any remaining marinade.

Meanwhile, in a small saucepan cook the green beans, uncovered, in a small amount of boiling water about 15 minutes or until crisp-tender. Drain beans.

To serve, divide the shredded mixed greens between 2 salad plates. Slice each chicken breast crosswise into 6 to 8 pieces. Reassemble chicken breasts on greens. Arrange cooked beans, orange slices, and mango slices on greens. Shake the reserved vinaigrette well; drizzle some over each serving. If desired, sprinkle with chopped peanuts or sesame seed. Makes 2 servings.

Cilantro Vinaigrette: In a screw-top jar combine ¼ cup *papaya* or *apricot nectar,* 3 tablespoons snipped *cilantro,* 2 tablespoons *olive oil* or *salad oil,* 2 tablespoons *rice wine vinegar* or *white wine vinegar,* 1 teaspoon toasted *sesame oil,* ½ teaspoon ground *ginger,* and ⅛ to ¼ teaspoon *ground red pepper.* Cover and shake well. Store vinaigrette in the refrigerator for up to 2 weeks. Shake well before serving. Makes about ½ cup.

Nutrition information per serving: 427 calories, 25 g protein, 37 g carbohydrate, 22 g fat (4 g saturated), 59 mg cholesterol, 78 mg sodium.

Garlic-Ginger Chicken Strip Salad

If you're watching your sodium, switch to reduced-sodium soy sauce.

4 small skinless, boneless chicken breast halves (about 12 ounces total)
¼ cup soy sauce
¼ cup dry sherry
1 tablespoon snipped fresh basil or 1 teaspoon dried basil, crushed
1 tablespoon honey
2 teaspoons grated gingerroot
½ teaspoon crushed red pepper
½ teaspoon black pepper
¼ teaspoon five-spice powder
4 cloves garlic, minced
2 cups broccoli flowerets
5 cups torn mixed greens
1 cup enoki mushrooms or sliced fresh mushrooms
1 medium red sweet pepper, cut into ¾-inch pieces (1 cup)
1 cup coarsely chopped red cabbage
Oriental Salad Dressing
Leaf lettuce

Rinse chicken; pat dry. Cut breast halves into bite-size strips. For marinade, in a medium mixing bowl combine soy sauce, sherry, basil, honey, gingerroot, crushed red pepper, black pepper, five-spice powder, and garlic. Add chicken strips; stir to coat. Cover and marinate in the refrigerator for 4 to 24 hours.

Drain chicken strips, reserving marinade. Place chicken on unheated rack of a broiler pan. Broil 4 to 5 inches from heat about 5 minutes or until light brown, brushing once with reserved marinade. Turn and brush again. Broil 3 to 5 minutes more or until chicken is tender and no longer pink. Discard remaining marinade.

Meanwhile, in a covered medium saucepan cook the broccoli in a small amount of boiling water for 1 minute. Drain well and chill.

In a large mixing bowl toss together torn mixed greens, mushrooms, red sweet pepper, red cabbage, and cooked broccoli. Shake Oriental Salad Dressing well. Pour about ½ cup of the dressing over greens mixture; toss lightly to coat. Line 4 salad plates with leaf lettuce. Divide greens mixture among salad plates. Top with chicken strips. Drizzle remaining dressing over chicken. Makes 4 servings.

Oriental Salad Dressing: In a screw-top jar combine ⅓ cup unsweetened *pineapple juice,* ¼ cup *rice vinegar* or *white vinegar,* 1 tablespoon *soy sauce,* 2 teaspoons *sugar,* 1½ teaspoons toasted *sesame oil,* and ¼ teaspoon *black pepper.* Cover and shake well. Makes ⅔ cup.

Nutrition information per serving: 235 calories, 21 g protein, 26 g carbohydrate, 5 g fat (1 g saturated), 45 mg cholesterol, 1,368 mg sodium.

Turkey and Fruit Pasta Salad

Savor this refreshing honey-dressed salad in the summertime when nectarines are at their peak.

1 cup packaged dried rope macaroni (gemelli) or 1⅓ cups corkscrew macaroni (4 ounces)

1½ cups chopped cooked turkey or chicken or fully cooked turkey ham (8 ounces)

2 green onions, sliced (¼ cup)

⅓ cup lime or lemon juice

¼ cup salad oil

1 tablespoon honey

2 teaspoons snipped fresh thyme or ½ teaspoon dried thyme, crushed

2 medium nectarines or plums, sliced

1 cup halved fresh strawberries

Cook pasta according to package directions. Drain pasta; rinse with cold water. Drain again.

In a large mixing bowl combine pasta; turkey, chicken, or turkey ham; and green onions. Toss to mix.

For dressing, in a screw-top jar combine lime or lemon juice, oil, honey, and thyme. Cover and shake well. Pour dressing over pasta mixture; toss to coat. Cover and chill for 4 to 24 hours.

Just before serving, add the nectarines or plums and strawberries. Toss to mix. Makes 4 servings.

Nutrition information per serving: 393 calories, 21 g protein, 39 g carbohydrate, 17 g fat (3 g saturated), 43 mg cholesterol, 42 mg sodium.

Pasta for Salads

The secret to fresh-tasting pasta salads is to avoid overcooking. Pasta cooked to just the right stage is called *al dente,* which means "to the tooth" in Italian. At this point, the pasta has a firm texture and is slightly chewy.

Salmon Salad with Julienne Vegetables

Looking for a company-special dish? Not only does this broiled salmon salad look impressive, but it also has a sophisticated dressing accented with lemon and fresh herbs.

4 fresh or frozen salmon steaks, cut
   ¾ inch thick (about 1½ pounds)
½ teaspoon finely shredded lemon peel
⅓ cup lemon juice
¼ cup salad oil
2 tablespoons water
2 teaspoons sugar
2 teaspoons snipped fresh thyme or
   ½ teaspoon dried thyme, crushed
2 teaspoons snipped fresh oregano or
   ½ teaspoon dried oregano,
   crushed
½ teaspoon paprika
⅛ teaspoon black pepper
1 clove garlic, minced
2 medium carrots, cut into thin,
   bite-size strips (about 1¼ cups)
1 medium zucchini, cut into thin,
   bite-size strips (about 1¼ cups)
1 medium red sweet pepper, cut into
   thin, bite-size strips (about 1 cup)
¾ cup water
   Boston or Bibb lettuce leaves
   Lemon slices (optional)
   Fresh thyme sprigs (optional)

Thaw salmon, if frozen. For dressing, in screw-top jar combine lemon peel, juice, salad oil, the 2 tablespoons water, the sugar, snipped or dried thyme, oregano, paprika, black pepper, and garlic. Cover and shake well.

Rinse salmon; pat dry. Place salmon in a shallow dish. Pour ¼ cup of the dressing over salmon. Turn salmon once to coat with dressing. Cover and marinate in the refrigerator for 1 hour, turning salmon once or twice.

Meanwhile, in a medium saucepan combine carrots, zucchini, red sweet pepper, and the ¾ cup water. Bring to boiling; reduce heat. Cover and simmer about 3 minutes or until vegetables are just crisp-tender. Drain vegetables; transfer to a mixing bowl. Pour ¼ cup of the remaining dressing over cooked vegetables, tossing lightly to coat; set aside. Set aside remaining dressing.

Drain salmon, reserving marinade. Place salmon on the greased unheated rack of a broiler pan. Broil 4 inches from heat for 5 minutes. Using a wide spatula, carefully turn salmon over. Brush salmon with marinade. Broil for 3 to 7 minutes more or until salmon flakes easily with a fork.

Line 4 salad plates with lettuce leaves. Arrange vegetables on lettuce. Place salmon on vegetables. Serve with reserved dressing. If desired, garnish with lemon slices and thyme sprigs. Makes 4 servings.

Nutrition information per serving: 326 calories, 26 g protein, 13 g carbohydrate, 20 g fat (3 g saturated), 31 mg cholesterol, 130 mg sodium.

Salmon-Pasta Salad

Fold the salmon gently into the pasta mixture so it stays in nice big chunks.

 1 cup packaged dried corkscrew
     macaroni or medium shell
     macaroni
1½ cups broccoli flowerets
 4 ounces Gruyère or Swiss cheese,
     cut into thin, bite-size strips
 ¼ cup sliced radishes
 ⅔ cup mayonnaise or salad dressing
 1 tablespoon snipped fresh basil or
     1 teaspoon dried basil, crushed
 2 teaspoons white wine Worcestershire
     sauce
 ⅛ teaspoon garlic salt
 1 to 2 tablespoons milk
 1 15½-ounce can salmon, chilled
     Leaf lettuce
     Pineapple sage flowers (optional)

In a large saucepan cook pasta in boiling salted water for 9 minutes. Add broccoli; return to boiling. Cook about 4 minutes more or until pasta and broccoli are tender. Drain the pasta and broccoli; rinse with cold water. Drain again.

In a large mixing bowl combine cooked pasta-broccoli mixture, Gruyère or Swiss cheese, and radishes.

For dressing, in a small mixing bowl stir together the mayonnaise or salad dressing, basil, white wine Worcestershire sauce, and garlic salt. Stir in enough of the milk to make desired consistency. Pour dressing over pasta mixture. Toss lightly to mix. Cover and chill for 4 to 24 hours.

Before serving, if necessary, stir a little additional milk into the pasta mixture to moisten. Drain and flake salmon, discarding skin and bones. Fold salmon into salad mixture.

Line 4 salad plates with leaf lettuce. Divide the salmon mixture among plates. If desired, garnish with pineapple sage flowers. Makes 4 servings.

Nutrition information per serving: 641 calories, 36 g protein, 19 g carbohydrate, 47 g fat (12 g saturated), 101 mg cholesterol, 999 mg sodium.

Seafood Louis Salad

Using a blend of low-fat cottage cheese and fat-free milk, instead of the traditional mayonnaise and whipping cream, eliminates about 30 grams of fat and makes this classic salad guilt-free for fat-watchers.

1 6-ounce package frozen, peeled, cooked shrimp
½ cup low-fat cottage cheese
2 tablespoons fat-free milk
1 tablespoon tomato paste
2 tablespoons chopped red sweet pepper or diced pimiento
1 green onion, thinly sliced
⅛ teaspoon salt
⅛ teaspoon black pepper
6 cups torn romaine
1 cup shredded red cabbage
1 medium carrot, shredded (½ cup)
1 6-ounce can crabmeat, drained, flaked, and cartilage removed
2 tomatoes, cut into thin wedges
   Carrot curls (optional)

Thaw shrimp. For dressing, in a blender container or food processor bowl combine cottage cheese, milk, and tomato paste. Cover and blend or process until smooth. Transfer mixture to a small bowl. Stir in red pepper or pimiento, green onion, salt, black pepper, and enough additional fat-free milk to make dressing of desired consistency. Cover and chill till serving time.

In a large bowl toss together romaine, red cabbage, and shredded carrot. Divide among salad plates. Arrange shrimp, crabmeat, and tomatoes on each plate. Drizzle with dressing. If desired, garnish with carrot curls. Pass any remaining dressing. Makes 3 servings.

Nutrition information per serving: 207 calories, 31 g protein, 14 g carbohydrate, 3 g fat (1 g saturated), 171 mg cholesterol, 729 mg sodium.

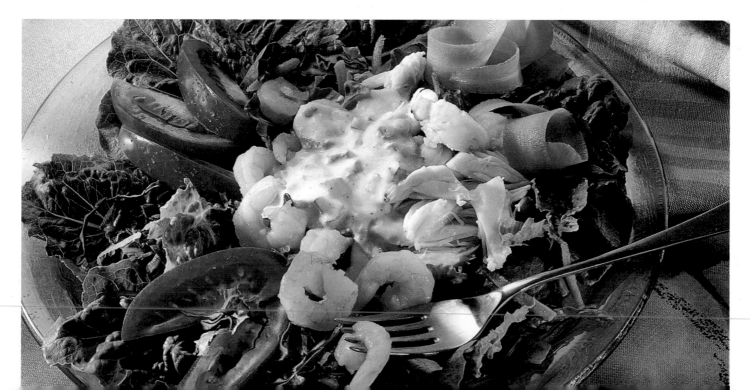

Grilled Vegetable Salad with Garlic Dressing

Vegetables, sweet and smoky from the grill, give pasta and cheese a jolt of flavor and color. By doing the grilling ahead, and storing the savory dressing in the refrigerator, this maximum-impact dish is done in the time it takes to simmer pasta.

---

2   red and/or yellow sweet peppers

2   Japanese eggplants, halved lengthwise

2   medium zucchini or yellow summer squash, halved lengthwise, or 8 to 10 yellow sunburst or pattypan squash*

1   tablespoon olive oil

2   cups packaged dried rigatoni or mostaccioli

    Roasted Garlic Dressing

¾   cup cubed fontina cheese (3 ounces)

1   to 2 tablespoons snipped Italian flat-leaf or curly parsley

    Italian flat-leaf parsley sprigs (optional)

Halve sweet peppers lengthwise; remove and discard stems, seeds, and membranes. Brush sweet peppers, eggplants, and squash with olive oil.

Grill vegetables on an uncovered grill directly over medium-hot coals for 8 to 12 minutes or until the vegetables are tender, turning occasionally. Remove vegetables from grill; cool slightly. Cut vegetables into 1-inch pieces.

Meanwhile, cook the pasta according to package directions. Drain pasta; rinse with cold water. Drain again. In a large bowl combine the pasta and grilled vegetables. Pour Roasted Garlic Dressing over pasta mixture. Toss gently to coat. Stir in fontina cheese. Sprinkle with snipped parsley. If desired, garnish with parsley sprigs. Makes 4 servings.

Roasted Garlic Dressing: In a screw-top jar combine 3 tablespoons *balsamic vinegar* or *red wine vinegar,* 2 tablespoons *olive oil,* 1 tablespoon *water,* 1 teaspoon bottled *roasted minced garlic,* ¼ teaspoon *salt,* and ¼ teaspoon *black pepper.* Cover and shake well.

*Note: If using sunburst or pattypan squash, cook the squash in a small amount of boiling water for 3 minutes before grilling.

Nutrition information per serving: 369 calories, 12 g protein, 40 g carbohydrate, 19 g fat (6 g saturated), 61 mg cholesterol, 317 mg sodium.

Texas-Style Bowls of Red

Texans have a high tolerance for hot and spicy foods, so if you're not from the Lone Star State, taste this extra-hot, authentic chili at your own risk!

20 small dried hot chile peppers or
    2 tablespoons crushed red pepper
2 dried ancho peppers or
    2 tablespoons chili powder
12 ounces beef round steak
12 ounces lean boneless pork
2 tablespoons cooking oil
1 cup chopped onion
1 tablespoon ground cumin
3 cloves garlic, minced
½ teaspoon paprika
¼ teaspoon black pepper
1 14½-ounce can beef broth
1 12-ounce can beer
3 cups hot cooked pinto beans and/or
    hot cooked rice
    Sliced jalapeño peppers (optional)

Crush hot chile peppers (if using). Remove stems and seeds from ancho peppers (if using); cut into 1-inch pieces. Place hot peppers and ancho peppers in a blender container or food processor bowl. Cover and blend or process until ground. Let pepper dust settle before opening blender or food processor. (If using crushed red pepper and chili powder, stir them together.) Set aside.

Trim fat from meat. Cut into ½-inch cubes. In a large saucepan or Dutch oven cook half of the meat in hot oil until brown. Remove meat and set aside. Add the remaining meat, onion, cumin, garlic, paprika, black pepper, and ground hot pepper or chili powder mixture. Cook until meat is brown. Return all meat to saucepan. Add beef broth and beer.

Bring to boiling; reduce heat. Cover and simmer for 45 minutes. Uncover and simmer about 30 minutes more or until meat is tender and broth mixture is desired consistency, stirring occasionally. Serve with hot cooked pinto beans and/or rice. If desired, garnish with jalapeño peppers. Makes 6 servings.

Nutrition information per serving: 340 calories, 26 g protein, 34 g carbohydrate, 10 g fat (2 g saturated), 44 mg cholesterol, 445 mg sodium.

Tuscan Sausage and Bean Soup

By using the crockery cooker method, you can have a dynamite Italian-style dinner ready when you step in the door, even if you were on the go all day.

1¼ cups dry Great Northern beans
1¾ cups beef broth
½ cup chopped onion
1 clove garlic, minced
½ teaspoon dried Italian seasoning, crushed
12 ounces uncooked Italian sausage links, cut into ½-inch slices
1 medium yellow summer squash or zucchini, sliced (2 cups)
1 14½-ounce can Italian-style tomatoes, cut up
⅓ cup dry red wine or water
½ of a 10-ounce package frozen chopped spinach, thawed and well drained
Grated Parmesan cheese (optional)

Rinse beans. In a large saucepan or Dutch oven combine beans and 4 cups cold water. Bring to boiling; reduce heat. Simmer, uncovered, for 2 minutes. Remove from heat. Cover and let stand for 1 hour. (Or, place beans in water in pan. Cover and soak beans overnight.) Drain and rinse beans.

In the same pan combine beans, 4 cups fresh water, beef broth, onion, garlic, and Italian seasoning. Bring to boiling; reduce heat. Cover and simmer about 2 hours or until beans are tender.

Meanwhile, in a medium skillet cook sliced Italian sausage until brown. Drain well on paper towels. Add cooked sausage, yellow squash or zucchini, undrained tomatoes, and red wine or water to bean mixture. Bring to boiling; reduce heat. Cover and simmer about 5 minutes more or until squash is tender.

Stir in spinach. Heat through. If desired, sprinkle each serving with Parmesan cheese. Makes 4 or 5 servings.

Crockery-Cooker Directions: Rinse beans. In a large saucepan combine beans and 4 cups cold water. Simmer, uncovered, for 10 minutes; drain. Prepare sausage as above. In a 3½- to 4-quart crockery cooker combine beans, 4 cups fresh water, beef broth, onion, garlic, Italian seasoning, cooked sausage, squash, undrained tomatoes, and red wine or water. Cover and cook on low heat setting for 11 to 12 hours or until beans are tender. Just before serving, stir spinach into soup. If desired, sprinkle each serving with cheese.

Nutrition information per serving: 563 calories, 36 g protein, 63 g carbohydrate, 19 g fat (6 g saturated), 49 mg cholesterol, 1,155 mg sodium.

Italian Beef Soup

Italian Beef Soup

Keep the ingredients on hand for this easy soup and you'll always be prepared to whip up a hearty supper.

1	pound lean ground beef
2	14½-ounce cans beef broth
3	cups frozen pasta with broccoli, corn, and carrots in garlic seasoned sauce
1	14½-ounce can diced tomatoes
1	5½-ounce can tomato juice or ⅔ cup no-salt-added tomato juice
2	teaspoons dried Italian seasoning, crushed
¼	cup grated Parmesan cheese

In a large saucepan cook ground beef until brown. Drain fat. Stir in beef broth, pasta with vegetables, undrained tomatoes, tomato juice, and Italian seasoning.

Bring to boiling; reduce heat. Simmer, uncovered, about 10 minutes or until vegetables and pasta are tender. Ladle into soup bowls. Sprinkle each serving with Parmesan cheese. Makes 6 servings.

Nutrition information per serving: 258 calories, 20 g protein, 13 g carbohydrate, 14 g fat (6 g saturated), 54 mg cholesterol, 929 mg sodium.

Easy Hamburger-Vegetable Soup

For a simple garnish, sprinkle with bite-size cheese or rich round crackers.

1	pound lean ground beef or pork
½	cup chopped onion
½	cup chopped green sweet pepper
4	cups beef broth
1	cup frozen whole kernel corn
1	7½-ounce can tomatoes, cut up
½	of a 9-ounce package frozen lima beans
½	cup chopped, peeled potato or ½ cup frozen hash brown potatoes
1	medium carrot, cut into julienne strips (½ cup)
1	tablespoon snipped fresh basil or 1 teaspoon dried basil, crushed
1	bay leaf
1	teaspoon Worcestershire sauce
⅛	teaspoon black pepper

In a large saucepan or Dutch oven cook ground meat, onion, and green pepper until meat is brown and onion is tender. Drain fat. Stir in beef broth, corn, undrained tomatoes, lima beans, potato, carrot, basil, bay leaf, Worcestershire sauce, and black pepper.

Bring to boiling; reduce heat. Cover and simmer for 15 to 20 minutes or until vegetables are tender. Discard bay leaf. Makes 4 servings.

Nutrition information per serving: 309 calories, 28 g protein, 25 g carbohydrate, 12 g fat (5 g saturated), 71 mg cholesterol, 958 mg sodium.

Mexican Chicken-Tortilla Soup

This soup features cilantro, a fresh herb that looks like a flattened parsley leaf but has a pungent, almost musty odor and taste that gives a distinctive flavor to Mexican dishes.

2 whole small chicken breasts
(about 1¼ pounds total)
3½ cups chicken broth
½ cup chopped onion
1 clove garlic, minced
½ teaspoon ground cumin
1 tablespoon cooking oil
1 14½-ounce can tomatoes, cut up
1 8-ounce can tomato sauce
1 4-ounce can whole green chile
peppers, rinsed, seeded, and cut
into thin bite-size strips
¼ cup snipped cilantro or parsley
1 tablespoon snipped fresh oregano or
1 teaspoon dried oregano, crushed
6 6-inch corn tortillas
Cooking oil
1 cup shredded cheddar or Monterey
Jack cheese (4 ounces)

Rinse chicken. In a large saucepan or Dutch oven combine chicken and chicken broth. Bring to boiling; reduce heat. Cover and simmer about 15 minutes or until chicken is tender and no longer pink. Remove chicken. Set aside to cool. Skin, bone, and finely shred chicken. Set chicken aside. Discard skin and bones. Strain broth through a large sieve or colander lined with two layers of 100% cotton cheesecloth. Skim fat from broth and set broth aside.

In the same saucepan cook onion, garlic, and cumin in 1 tablespoon hot oil until onion is tender. Stir in strained broth, undrained tomatoes, tomato sauce, chile peppers, cilantro or parsley, and oregano. Bring to boiling; reduce heat. Cover and simmer for 20 minutes. Stir in shredded chicken. Heat through.

Meanwhile, cut tortillas in half, then cut crosswise into ½-inch-wide strips. In a heavy medium skillet heat ¼ inch oil. Cook strips in hot oil, half at a time, about 1 minute or until crisp and light brown. Remove with a slotted spoon; drain on paper towels.

Divide fried tortilla strips among soup bowls. Ladle soup over tortilla strips. Sprinkle each serving with shredded cheese. Serve immediately. Makes 4 servings.

Nutrition information per serving: 496 calories, 38 g protein, 33 g carbohydrate, 24 g fat (8 g saturated), 85 mg cholesterol, 1,658 mg sodium.

Cream of Chile-Chicken Soup

Ground red pepper and green chile peppers add a spiciness to this creamy soup. For an accompaniment, serve some cornbread or cornsticks with it.

8 ounces ground raw chicken or turkey

¼ cup chopped onion

2 cloves garlic, minced

2 cups milk

1 10¾-ounce can condensed cream of chicken soup

1 7-ounce can whole kernel corn with sweet peppers, drained

1 medium tomato, chopped (¾ cup)

1 4-ounce can diced green chile peppers, drained

2 tablespoons snipped cilantro or parsley

¼ teaspoon ground red pepper

1 cup shredded Monterey Jack cheese (4 ounces)

In a large saucepan or Dutch oven cook ground chicken or turkey, onion, and garlic until chicken or turkey is no longer pink and onion is tender. Drain fat, if necessary.

Stir in milk, cream of chicken soup, corn, chopped tomato, chile peppers, cilantro or parsley, and ground red pepper. Bring to boiling; reduce heat. Simmer, uncovered, for 5 minutes, stirring occasionally.

Add Monterey Jack cheese. Cook and stir until cheese is melted. Makes 4 servings.

Nutrition information per serving: 375 calories, 24 g protein, 29 g carbohydrate, 19 g fat (9 g saturated), 68 mg cholesterol, 1,481 mg sodium.

BROTH OPTIONS

Many of the recipes in this chapter call for chicken broth, beef broth, or vegetable broth. If you're fresh out of canned broth, you can use bouillon granules or cubes as an easy substitute. Just remember that 1 cup of canned broth is equivalent to 1 teaspoon of granules or 1 cube dissolved in 1 cup water. Look for canned broth and bouillon granules or cubes with the soups at your supermarket.

Chunky Vegetable-Cod Soup

This fish soup will win your family's approval … hook, line, and sinker!

1	pound fresh or frozen skinless cod fillets or steaks
½	cup chopped red sweet pepper
¼	cup chopped onion
1	tablespoon margarine or butter
3½	cups vegetable broth or chicken broth
1	cup frozen cut green beans
1	cup coarsely chopped cabbage
½	cup sliced carrot
1	teaspoon snipped fresh basil
1	teaspoon snipped fresh thyme
½	teaspoon snipped fresh rosemary
¼	teaspoon black pepper
	Lemon wedges (optional)

Thaw fish, if frozen. Rinse fish. Cut into 1-inch pieces. In a large saucepan or Dutch oven cook red pepper and onion in margarine or butter until tender.

Stir in the broth, green beans, cabbage, carrot, basil, thyme, rosemary, and black pepper. Bring to boiling; reduce heat. Cover and simmer for 8 to 10 minutes or until vegetables are nearly tender.

Stir fish into broth mixture. Return to boiling; reduce heat. Cover and simmer about 5 minutes or until fish flakes easily with a fork, stirring once. If desired, serve with lemon wedges. Makes 4 servings.

Nutrition information per serving: 140 calories, 20 g protein, 9 g carbohydrate, 5 g fat (1 g saturated), 45 mg cholesterol, 922 mg sodium.

Manhattan Fish Chowder

Manhattan-style chowders are tomato-based and may contain other vegetables in place of the potatoes found in milk-based New England-style chowders.

12	ounces fresh or frozen fish fillets
1	24-ounce can vegetable juice
1	11-ounce can whole kernel corn with sweet peppers
½	cup sliced green onions
¼	cup chicken broth
1½	teaspoons snipped fresh thyme or ½ teaspoon dried thyme, crushed
1	teaspoon Worcestershire sauce
	Several dashes bottled hot pepper sauce

Thaw fish, if frozen. Rinse fish. Cut fish into ¾-inch pieces. In a large saucepan combine vegetable juice, corn, green onions, broth, thyme, Worcestershire sauce, and hot pepper sauce. Bring to boiling; reduce heat. Cover and simmer for 8 minutes.

Stir fish into juice mixture. Return to boiling; reduce heat. Cover and simmer for 3 to 5 minutes more or until fish flakes easily with a fork, stirring once. Makes 4 servings.

Nutrition information per serving: 164 calories, 16 g protein, 22 g carbohydrate, 1 g fat (0 g saturated), 34 mg cholesterol, 995 mg sodium.

Chunky Vegetable-Cod Soup

Hearty Bean and Rice Soup

Arborio rice is an Italian-grown grain that is shorter and plumper than any other short-grain rice; it adds a creamy texture to this bean and vegetable soup.

2	stalks celery, finely chopped
1	large onion, finely chopped
2	cloves garlic, minced
1	tablespoon olive oil
5	cups beef broth
1	cup water
½	cup Arborio rice
6	cups torn spinach
1	15-ounce can Great Northern beans, rinsed and drained
3	medium tomatoes, chopped
1	medium zucchini, chopped
¼	cup snipped fresh thyme
¼	teaspoon cracked pepper
	Spinach leaves (optional)
½	cup crumbled feta cheese

In a Dutch oven cook celery, onion, and garlic in hot oil until tender. Add beef broth, water, and uncooked rice. Bring to boiling; reduce heat. Cover and simmer for 15 minutes.

Stir in torn spinach, Great Northern beans, tomatoes, zucchini, thyme, and cracked pepper. Cook and stir until heated through. If desired, garnish with additional spinach leaves. Sprinkle each serving with feta cheese. Makes 6 servings.

Nutrition information per serving: 252 calories, 13 g protein, 39 g carbohydrate, 6 g fat (2 g saturated), 8 mg cholesterol, 834 mg sodium.

Potato-Bean Soup

To save about 150 mg of sodium per serving, use reduced-sodium chicken broth.

2	medium carrots, shredded (1 cup)
½	cup sliced celery
1	clove garlic, minced
1	tablespoon margarine or butter
4	cups chicken broth
3	cups cubed, peeled potatoes
2	teaspoons dried dillweed
1	15-ounce can white kidney (cannellini) beans, rinsed and drained
½	cup dairy sour cream
1	tablespoon all-purpose flour
⅛	teaspoon pepper

In a large saucepan cook carrots, celery, and garlic in margarine or butter until tender. Stir in broth, potatoes, and dillweed. Cover and simmer for 20 to 25 minutes or until potatoes are tender. With back of a spoon, slightly mash about half of the potatoes against side of pan. Stir in white kidney beans.

In a small bowl stir together sour cream, flour, and pepper; stir into potato mixture. Cook and stir until bubbly. Cook and stir for 1 minute more. Makes 4 to 6 servings.

Nutrition information per serving: 296 calories, 14 g protein, 42 g carbohydrate, 11 g fat (5 g saturated), 13 mg cholesterol, 1,031 mg sodium.

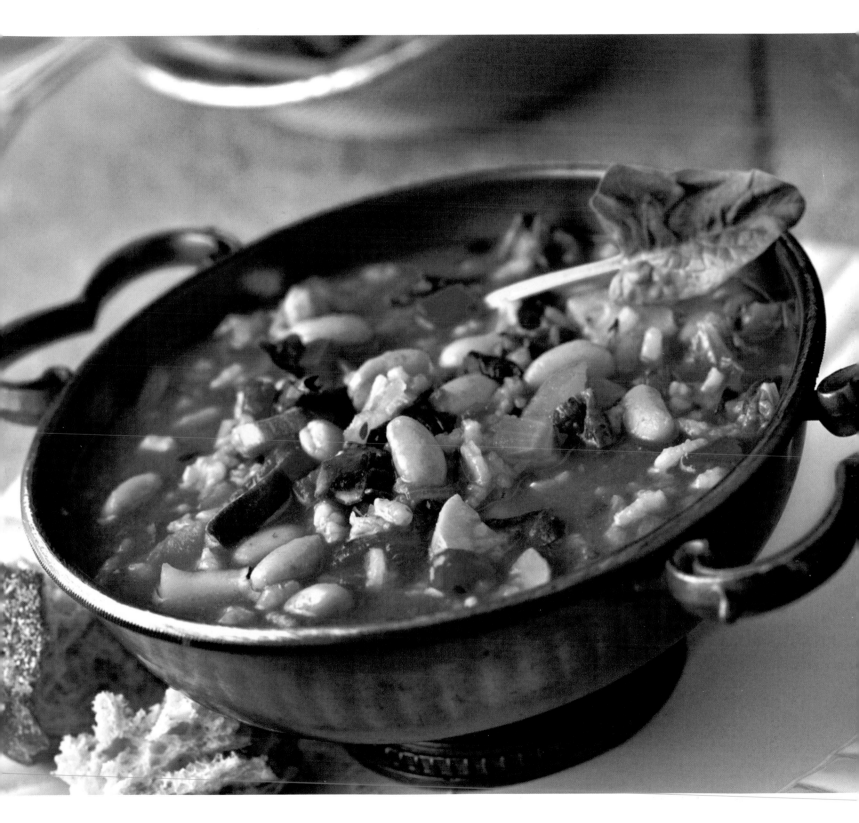

Hearty Bean and Rice Soup

Minestrone

The countless versions of this classic Italian soup all have one thing in common—they're full of beans, pasta, and vegetables.

2   14½-ounce cans chicken broth or beef broth
1   14½-ounce can tomatoes, cut up
1   cup chopped onion
1   cup shredded cabbage
¾   cup tomato juice
½   cup chopped carrot
½   cup sliced celery
1   tablespoon snipped fresh basil or 1 teaspoon dried basil, crushed
¼   teaspoon garlic powder
1   15-ounce can white kidney (cannellini) beans or Great Northern beans, rinsed and drained
1   medium zucchini, sliced ¼ inch thick (1 cup)
½   of a 9-ounce package frozen Italian-style green beans
2   ounces packaged dried spaghetti or linguine, broken (about ½ cup)
2   tablespoons shaved or finely shredded Parmesan cheese

In a Dutch oven combine broth, undrained tomatoes, onion, cabbage, tomato juice, carrot, celery, basil, and garlic powder. Bring to boiling; reduce heat. Cover and simmer for 20 minutes.

Stir in white kidney or Great Northern beans, zucchini, green beans, and pasta. Return to boiling; reduce heat. Cover and simmer for 10 to 15 minutes more or until vegetables and pasta are tender.

Ladle into soup bowls. Sprinkle each serving with Parmesan cheese. Makes 4 servings.

Nutrition information per serving: 243 calories, 17 g protein, 44 g carbohydrate, 3 g fat (1 g saturated), 2 mg cholesterol, 1,315 mg sodium.

Tomato Tactics

To quickly cut up canned tomatoes, leave them in the can and use kitchen shears or scissors to snip them into small pieces. When a recipe calls for using both the cut-up tomatoes and their juice, there's no need to drain the tomatoes.

Beef & PORK

Contents

GARLIC-SAGE-MARINATED BEEF
POT ROAST (recipe, page 75)

Garlic Steaks with Nectarine-Onion Relish

What's better than the smell of steak on the grill in the summertime? The aroma of garlic-studded beef on the grill. Serve this steak with some crusty bread to soak up the delicious juices.

4 boneless beef top loin steaks, cut
    1 inch thick
6 cloves garlic, thinly sliced
2 medium onions, coarsely chopped
1 teaspoon olive oil
2 tablespoons cider vinegar
1 tablespoon honey
1 medium nectarine, chopped
2 teaspoons snipped fresh applemint,
    pineapplemint, or spearmint
    Fresh applemint, pineapplemint,
    or spearmint sprigs (optional)

Trim fat from steaks. With the point of a paring knife, make small slits in steaks. Insert half of the garlic slices into slits.

Wrap the steaks in plastic wrap; let stand at room temperature up to 20 minutes. (For more intense flavor, chill steaks up to 8 hours.) Sprinkle the steaks with salt and pepper.

Meanwhile, for relish, in a large nonstick skillet cook onions and remaining garlic in hot oil over medium heat about 10 minutes or until onions are a deep golden color (but not brown), stirring occasionally. Stir in vinegar and honey. Stir in nectarine and the snipped mint. Heat through.

Grill steaks on an uncovered grill directly over medium coals to desired doneness, turning once. (Allow 8 to 12 minutes for medium rare or 12 to 15 minutes for medium.) Serve the relish with steaks. If desired, garnish with mint sprigs. Makes 4 servings.

Nutrition information per serving: 272 calories, 34 g protein, 13 g carbohydrate, 9 g fat (3 g saturated), 97 mg cholesterol, 108 mg sodium.

Olive Oil Options

All olive oils are not the same. This versatile oil, made from pressed olives, is sold by grade from "pure" (a blend of lower- and higher-quality oils) to "extra virgin" (the richest in aroma and flavor). Color also indicates a flavor difference. Green to greenish gold olive oil tastes slightly sharp. Golden olive oil has a more delicate flavor.

Peppered Steak with Mushroom Gravy

Tenderloin is one of the leanest cuts of beef. To keep these prized steaks at their moist and juicy best, don't overcook them.

6 beef tenderloin steaks or 3 beef top loin steaks, cut 1 inch thick (about 1½ pounds total)

1½ teaspoons dried whole green peppercorns, crushed, or ½ teaspoon coarsely ground black pepper

½ teaspoon dried thyme, crushed

½ teaspoon dried oregano, crushed

¼ teaspoon salt
Nonstick spray coating

⅓ cup water

½ teaspoon instant beef bouillon granules

¾ cup sliced fresh shiitake mushrooms or other fresh mushrooms

¾ cup fat-free milk

2 tablespoons all-purpose flour

½ teaspoon dried thyme, crushed

⅔ cup fat-free or light dairy sour cream
Fresh thyme sprigs (optional)

Trim fat from steaks. In a small bowl stir together the peppercorns or pepper, ½ teaspoon dried thyme, oregano, and salt. Sprinkle both sides of steaks with pepper mixture, pressing into meat.

Spray an unheated large nonstick skillet with nonstick coating. Preheat over medium heat. Add steaks and cook to desired doneness, turning once. (Allow 8 to 11 minutes for medium rare or 12 to 14 minutes for medium.) Remove from skillet. Cover and keep warm.

For sauce, add water and bouillon granules to skillet. Bring to boiling. Add the mushrooms. Cook about 2 minutes or until tender. Stir together milk, flour, and ½ teaspoon dried thyme. Add to mushroom mixture. Cook and stir until thickened and bubbly. Stir in sour cream. Heat through, but do not boil.

To serve, spoon the sauce over steaks. If desired, garnish with fresh thyme. Makes 6 servings.

Nutrition information per serving: 206 calories, 25 g protein, 9 g carbohydrate, 7 g fat (3 g saturated), 64 mg cholesterol, 243 mg sodium.

Oriental Family Steak

Oriental Family Steak

To ensure a tender steak, marinate the meat at least 8 hours, and slice it as thin as you can.

1	1½- to 2-pound beef top round steak, cut 1 inch thick
⅓	cup soy sauce
⅓	cup dry sherry
2	green onions, thinly sliced
1	tablespoon brown sugar
1	clove garlic, minced
½	teaspoon dry mustard
⅛	teaspoon ground ginger
	Soy sauce (optional)

Trim fat from meat. Place meat in a plastic bag and set the bag into a shallow dish. For marinade, combine ⅓ cup soy sauce, sherry, green onions, brown sugar, garlic, mustard, and ginger. Pour over meat; seal bag. Marinate in the refrigerator for 8 to 24 hours, turning bag occasionally. Drain meat, reserving marinade.

In a covered grill arrange medium-hot coals around a drip pan. Test for medium heat above pan. Place meat on grill rack over drip pan. Cover and grill to desired doneness. (Allow 24 to 26 minutes for medium rare or 28 to 30 minutes for medium.) Brush occasionally with marinade up to the last 5 minutes of grilling.

Cut the meat into thin slices. If desired, serve with additional soy sauce. Makes 6 to 8 servings.

Nutrition information per serving: 185 calories, 28 g protein, 3 g carbohydrate, 5 g fat (2 g saturated), 72 mg cholesterol, 512 mg sodium.

Herb-Pepper Sirloin Steak

A mixture of catsup, herbs, and pepper coats both sides of this steak, complementing the hearty beef flavor.

1	1½-pound boneless beef sirloin steak, cut 1 inch thick
2	tablespoons catsup
1½	teaspoons snipped fresh rosemary or ½ teaspoon dried rosemary, crushed
1½	teaspoons snipped fresh basil or ½ teaspoon dried basil, crushed
½	teaspoon coarsely ground pepper
⅛	teaspoon garlic powder
⅛	teaspoon ground cardamom (optional)

Trim fat from steak. Combine catsup, rosemary, basil, pepper, garlic powder, and, if desired, cardamom. Coat both sides of steak with catsup mixture.

Grill steak on an uncovered grill directly over medium coals to desired doneness, turning once. (Allow 14 to 18 minutes for medium rare or 18 to 22 minutes for medium.) Cut steak into serving-size pieces. Makes 6 servings.

Nutrition information per serving: 208 calories, 26 g protein, 2 g carbohydrate, 10 g fat (4 g saturated), 76 mg cholesterol, 124 mg sodium.

Midwest Swiss Steak with Tomato Gravy

Serve this satisfying entrée with a tossed green salad and crusty sourdough rolls.

1½	pounds boneless beef round steak
2	tablespoons all-purpose flour
	Nonstick spray coating
2	large onions, sliced
2	cups chopped peeled parsnips
1	14½-ounce can low-sodium tomatoes, cut up
1	large red sweet pepper, chopped
1	cup beef broth
1	teaspoon salt-free seasoning blend
1	teaspoon dried basil, crushed
1	clove garlic, minced
¼	teaspoon black pepper
1	tablespoon cold water
1	teaspoon cornstarch
2	tablespoons snipped parsley

Trim fat from meat. Cut the meat into 6 serving-size pieces. Sprinkle both sides of the meat with flour. With a meat mallet, pound the flour into the meat.

Spray an unheated 12-inch skillet with nonstick coating. Preheat over medium heat. Add meat and cook until brown on both sides. Add the onions, parsnips, undrained tomatoes, sweet pepper, beef broth, seasoning blend, basil, garlic, and black pepper.

Bring to boiling; reduce heat. Cover and simmer about 1¼ hours or until meat and vegetables are tender. Transfer meat and vegetables to a platter. Cover and keep warm while preparing sauce.

For sauce, skim fat from pan drippings. Stir together water and cornstarch. Stir into pan drippings. Cook and stir until thickened and bubbly. Cook and stir for 2 minutes more. Stir in parsley. Serve sauce over meat and vegetables. Makes 6 servings.

Nutrition information per serving: 211 calories, 25 g protein, 16 g carbohydrate, 5 g fat (2 g saturated), 60 mg cholesterol, 321 mg sodium.

Snipping Savvy

Snipping parsley and other fresh herbs takes only a few moments. Loosely pack the cleaned and dried leaves in a glass measuring cup. Use kitchen shears to cut them into small uniform pieces. This method eliminates the work of washing a cutting board.

Garlic-Sage-Marinated Beef Pot Roast

Red wine, tomato paste, and garlic give this fork-tender roast a robust, well-rounded flavor.

1 2- to 2½-pound boneless beef chuck
   pot roast
¾ cup dry red wine or tomato juice
2 tablespoons tomato paste
1 tablespoon snipped fresh sage or
   ½ teaspoon ground sage
10 cloves garlic, halved
2 teaspoons instant beef bouillon
   granules
¼ teaspoon pepper
1 tablespoon cooking oil
1¼ pounds tiny new potatoes or
   4 medium potatoes
4 medium carrots, cut into 2-inch
   pieces
2 small onions, cut into wedges
2 stalks celery, bias-sliced into
   1-inch pieces
½ cup cold water
¼ cup all-purpose flour

Trim fat from meat. Place meat in a plastic bag and set the bag into a shallow dish. For marinade, in a small bowl combine the red wine or tomato juice, tomato paste, sage, garlic, beef bouillon granules, and pepper. Pour over meat; seal bag. Marinate in the refrigerator for 6 to 24 hours, turning bag occasionally. Drain meat, reserving the marinade.

In a Dutch oven brown the meat on both sides in hot oil. Drain fat. Pour the marinade over meat. Bring to boiling; reduce heat. Cover and simmer for 1 hour.

Remove a narrow strip of peel from around the center of each new potato. (Or, peel and quarter each medium potato.) Add potatoes, carrots, onions, and celery to meat. Cover and simmer for 45 to 60 minutes or until meat and vegetables are tender, adding some water if necessary. Transfer meat and vegetables to a platter. Cover and keep warm while preparing gravy.

For gravy, measure pan juices; skim fat. If necessary, add water to equal 1¾ cups liquid; return to Dutch oven. Combine the ½ cup water and flour; stir into juices. Cook and stir until thickened and bubbly. Cook and stir for 1 minute more. Season to taste with salt and pepper. Serve gravy with meat and vegetables. Makes 8 servings.

Nutrition information per serving: 321 calories, 29 g protein, 28 g carbohydrate, 8 g fat (3 g saturated), 78 mg cholesterol, 345 mg sodium.

Beef Fajitas

For chicken fajitas, substitute skinless, boneless chicken breast halves for the flank steak.

1 1½-pound beef flank steak
¼ cup lime juice
2 tablespoons soy sauce
1 tablespoon cooking oil
1 clove garlic, minced
1 avocado, seeded, peeled, and
    coarsely chopped
¼ cup salsa
1 tablespoon snipped cilantro
1 tablespoon lime juice
¼ teaspoon bottled hot pepper sauce
12 8-inch flour tortillas
2 medium onions, sliced
2 medium green sweet peppers,
    cut into strips
1 tablespoon cooking oil
½ cup dairy sour cream
1 medium tomato, coarsely chopped
    (optional)

Trim fat from meat. Score meat by making shallow diagonal cuts at 1-inch intervals in a diamond pattern. Repeat on other side. Place meat in a plastic bag and set the bag into a shallow dish.

For marinade, in a small bowl combine ¼ cup lime juice, soy sauce, 1 tablespoon oil, and garlic. Pour over meat; seal bag. Marinate in the refrigerator for 6 to 12 hours, turning bag occasionally. Toss together the avocado, salsa, cilantro, 1 tablespoon lime juice, and pepper sauce. Cover and chill. Wrap tortillas in foil.

Fold a 36x18-inch piece of heavy foil in half to make an 18-inch square. Place onions and green peppers in center of foil. Drizzle with 1 tablespoon oil. Bring up two opposite edges of foil and seal with a double fold. Then fold remaining ends to completely enclose the vegetables, leaving space for steam to build.

Grill vegetable packet on an uncovered grill directly over medium coals for 10 minutes. Drain the meat, reserving marinade. Add the meat to grill.

Grill meat and vegetable packet for 6 minutes. Brush the meat with marinade; turn meat. Add the wrapped tortillas to grill. Grill for 6 to 8 minutes more or until meat is slightly pink in center and vegetables are crisp-tender.

To serve, thinly slice meat across the grain. Arrange meat, onions, and peppers on tortillas. Top with the avocado mixture, sour cream, and, if desired, tomato. Roll up tortillas around filling. Makes 6 servings.

Nutrition information per serving: 539 calories, 30 g protein, 49 g carbohydrate, 25 g fat (6 g saturated), 61 mg cholesterol, 604 mg sodium.

Sweet-and-Sour Steak

The sweet-and-sour dishes of Canton are among the most familiar types of Chinese food. They are said to have evolved in response to the demanding tastes of the foreigners in this large port city.

8   ounces beef top round steak
1   small orange
1   15¼-ounce can pineapple chunks
        (juice pack)
2   tablespoons vinegar
2   tablespoons soy sauce
1   tablespoon cornstarch
1   tablespoon brown sugar
⅛   teaspoon ground red pepper
1   tablespoon cooking oil
1   medium green sweet pepper, cut
        into 1-inch pieces
1   small onion, cut into thin wedges
2   cups hot cooked rice
        Orange slices (optional)

Trim fat from meat. Partially freeze meat. Thinly slice across the grain into bite-size strips. Set aside. Peel and section orange. Set aside.

For sauce, drain pineapple, reserving juice. Pour ½ cup of the reserved juice into a small bowl. (Reserve remaining juice for another use.) Stir in the vinegar, soy sauce, cornstarch, brown sugar, and ground red pepper. Set aside.

Add cooking oil to a wok or large skillet. Preheat over medium-high heat (add more oil if necessary during cooking). Stir-fry green pepper and onion in hot oil for 3 to 4 minutes or until crisp-tender. Remove the vegetables from wok.

Add meat to wok. Stir-fry for 2 to 3 minutes or until meat is slightly pink in center. Push meat from center of wok. Stir sauce; add to center of wok. Cook and stir until thickened and bubbly.

Return cooked vegetables to wok. Add pineapple chunks. Stir all ingredients together to coat. Cook and stir about 2 minutes more or until heated through. Stir in orange sections. Serve immediately over hot rice. If desired, garnish with orange slices. Makes 4 servings.

Nutrition information per serving: 326 calories, 17 g protein, 51 g carbohydrate, 7 g fat (2 g saturated fat), 36 mg cholesterol, 545 mg sodium.

Southwest Beef-Linguine Toss

A jar of picante sauce makes an easy, yet flavor-packed sauce in this one-dish meal.

4	ounces packaged dried linguine
12	ounces beef top round steak
1	tablespoon cooking oil
2	teaspoons chili powder
1	clove garlic, minced
1	small onion, sliced and separated into rings
1	red or green sweet pepper, cut into strips
1	10-ounce package frozen whole kernel corn
¼	cup picante sauce
	Cilantro sprigs (optional)

Cook pasta according to package directions. Drain pasta; rinse with warm water. Drain again. Meanwhile, trim fat from meat. Cut meat into thin, bite-size strips.

Add cooking oil to a wok or large skillet. Preheat over medium-high heat (add more oil if necessary during cooking). Stir-fry chili powder and garlic in hot oil for 15 seconds. Add onion; stir-fry for 1 minute. Add sweet pepper; stir-fry for 1 to 2 minutes more or until vegetables are crisp-tender. Remove from wok.

Add meat to wok. Stir-fry for 2 to 3 minutes or until meat is slightly pink in center. Return vegetables to wok. Stir in corn and picante sauce. Add the cooked pasta. Toss all ingredients together to coat. Cook and stir until heated through. Serve immediately. If desired, garnish with cilantro. Makes 4 servings.

Nutrition information per serving: 351 calories, 27 g protein, 43 g carbohydrate, 9 g fat (2 g saturated fat), 54 mg cholesterol, 166 mg sodium.

STIR-FRYING GARLIC

To evenly distribute garlic flavor to stir-fry ingredients, season the oil by cooking the garlic first. Cook the garlic in the hot oil, keeping it moving constantly so it doesn't burn. After about 15 seconds, begin adding the other stir-fry ingredients to the oil.

Double Salsa Burgers

A fresh tomato salsa flavors the beef mixture and also serves as a colorful topping for these zesty burgers.

1	large tomato, seeded and finely chopped
½	cup finely chopped green sweet pepper
¼	cup finely chopped red onion
2	jalapeño peppers, seeded and finely chopped
1	tablespoon snipped cilantro
1	clove garlic, minced
¼	teaspoon salt
1½	pounds lean ground beef
2	cups shredded lettuce
⅓	cup shredded cheddar cheese
¼	cup dairy sour cream and/or guacamole

For salsa, in a medium bowl combine tomato, green pepper, onion, jalapeño peppers, cilantro, garlic, and salt. Set aside 2 tablespoons of the salsa. Cover and chill the remaining salsa until serving time.

In another medium bowl combine ground beef and the 2 tablespoons salsa; mix well. Shape mixture into six ½-inch-thick oval patties.

Grill patties on an uncovered grill directly over medium coals for 12 to 14 minutes or until meat is done (160°), turning once.

Arrange shredded lettuce on dinner plates. Top with patties, remaining salsa, and cheddar cheese. Serve with sour cream and/or guacamole. Makes 6 servings.

Nutrition information per serving: 298 calories, 24 g protein, 6 g carbohydrate, 19 g fat (9 g saturated), 87 mg cholesterol, 350 mg sodium.

Handle with Care

Because hot peppers contain oils that can burn your eyes, lips, and skin, protect yourself when working with the peppers by covering one or both hands with plastic bags (or wear plastic gloves). Be sure to wash your hands thoroughly before touching your eyes or face.

Fusilli with Creamy Tomato and Meat Sauce

Whipping cream enriches this herbed tomato and meat sauce. Serve it over your favorite pasta strands.

12	ounces lean ground beef or ground raw turkey
1	large onion, chopped (1 cup)
2	cloves garlic, minced
2	14½-ounce cans peeled Italian-style tomatoes, cut up
1	teaspoon dried Italian seasoning, crushed
½	teaspoon sugar
¼	teaspoon salt
⅛	teaspoon pepper
8	ounces packaged dried fusilli, vermicelli, or spaghetti
½	cup whipping cream
2	tablespoons snipped parsley
	Fresh rosemary sprigs (optional)

For sauce, in a large saucepan cook beef or turkey, onion, and garlic until meat is brown. Drain fat. Stir in the undrained tomatoes, Italian seasoning, sugar, salt, and pepper. Bring to boiling; reduce heat. Simmer, uncovered, about 40 minutes or until most of the liquid has evaporated, stirring occasionally.

Meanwhile, cook the pasta according to package directions. Drain; keep warm.

Gradually stir the whipping cream into the sauce. Heat through, stirring constantly. Remove from heat. Stir in parsley.

Arrange the pasta on dinner plates or a large platter. Spoon the sauce over the pasta. If desired, garnish with fresh rosemary sprigs. Makes 4 servings.

Nutrition information per serving: 523 calories, 26 g protein, 59 g carbohydrate, 21 g fat (10 g saturated), 94 mg cholesterol, 534 mg sodium.

𝒫IPING HOT PASTA

To keep pasta warm, return the hot drained pasta to the hot cooking pan and cover it. To avoid overcooking the pasta and to prevent sticking, hold the hot pasta no longer than 10 minutes and stir it once or twice.

Easy Taco Pizza

This hearty south-of-the border pizza is popular with both kids and adults alike.

Cornmeal Pizza Dough
12 ounces lean ground beef
1 cup chopped onion
1 8-ounce can tomato sauce
1 2¼-ounce can sliced pitted ripe olives, drained
1 1¼-ounce envelope taco seasoning mix
2 cups shredded cheddar cheese (8 ounces)
2 cups shredded lettuce
2 cups chopped tomatoes
2 medium avocados, seeded, peeled, and chopped
1 8-ounce carton dairy sour cream
Chili powder (optional)

Prepare Cornmeal Pizza Dough. Grease two 11- to 13-inch pizza pans or baking sheets. On a lightly floured surface, roll each half of dough into a circle 1 inch larger than pizza pan. Transfer dough to pans. Build up edges slightly. If desired, flute edges. Prick crusts well with a fork. Do not let rise. Bake in a 425° oven for 10 to 12 minutes or until crusts are lightly browned.

Meanwhile, in a large skillet cook ground beef and onion until meat is brown and onion is tender. Drain fat. Stir in tomato sauce, olives, and taco seasoning mix. Heat through.

Spread meat mixture over hot crusts. Sprinkle with cheese. Bake about 12 minutes more or until cheese is melted. Top with lettuce, tomatoes, avocados, and sour cream. If desired, sprinkle sour cream with chili powder. Makes 6 servings.

Cornmeal Pizza Dough: In a large bowl combine 1¼ cups *all-purpose flour*, 1 package *active dry yeast*, and ¼ teaspoon *salt*. Add 1 cup *warm water* (120° to 130°) and 2 tablespoons *cooking oil*. Beat with an electric mixer on low speed for 30 seconds. Beat on high speed for 3 minutes. Using a spoon, stir in ¾ cup *yellow cornmeal* and as much of ¾ to 1¼ cups additional *all-purpose flour* as you can. On a lightly floured surface, knead in enough of the remaining flour to make a moderately stiff dough that is smooth and elastic (6 to 8 minutes total). Divide in half. Cover and let rest for 10 minutes.

Nutrition information per serving: 726 calories, 32 g protein, 56 g carbohydrate, 45 g fat (15 g saturated), 90 mg cholesterol, 1,274 mg sodium.

Chili Macaroni

Wagon wheel macaroni and green beans replace the kidney beans in this chili-style dish.

12	ounces lean ground beef or ground raw turkey
1	medium onion, chopped (½ cup)
1	14½-ounce can Mexican-style stewed tomatoes
1¼	cups tomato juice
2	tablespoons canned diced green chile peppers, drained
2	teaspoons chili powder
½	teaspoon garlic salt
1	cup packaged dried wagon wheel macaroni or elbow macaroni
1	cup loose-pack frozen cut green beans
1	cup shredded cheddar cheese (4 ounces)

In a large skillet cook the ground beef or turkey and onion until meat is brown. Drain fat.

Stir stewed tomatoes, tomato juice, chile peppers, chili powder, and garlic salt into the meat mixture. Bring to boiling. Stir in pasta and green beans. Return to boiling; reduce heat. Cover and simmer about 15 minutes or until pasta and beans are tender.

To serve, spoon into bowls. Sprinkle each serving with shredded cheddar cheese. Makes 4 servings.

Nutrition information per serving: 427 calories, 29 g protein, 32 g carbohydrate, 21 g fat (10 g saturated), 83 mg cholesterol, 1,118 mg sodium.

SELECTING GROUND BEEF

For lower-fat cooking, choose the leanest ground beef possible. Ground beef can range in fat from 75 percent lean (25 percent fat) to 97 percent lean (3 percent fat). For soups, stews, tacos, or casseroles, use 95 to 97 percent lean ground beef. Because very lean ground beef tends to crumble and be less juicy, you may want to use ground beef with slightly more fat for meat loaves, burgers, and meatballs.

Plum Good Pork Chops

Plum Good Pork Chops

Plum preserves make this glistening glaze simple to make. Try it with grilled chicken or lamb, too.

3	tablespoons plum preserves
1	green onion, thinly sliced
1	tablespoon soy sauce
2	teaspoons lemon juice
⅛	teaspoon curry powder
	Dash ground cinnamon
	Dash ground red pepper
4	pork loin or rib chops, cut 1¼ inches thick (about 2 pounds total)
1	clove garlic, halved
	Plum wedges (optional)

For sauce, in a small saucepan heat and stir plum preserves, green onion, soy sauce, lemon juice, curry powder, cinnamon, and red pepper over medium heat until bubbly. Trim fat from chops. Rub both sides of chops with cut sides of garlic.

Grill chops on an uncovered grill directly over medium coals for 25 to 30 minutes or until slightly pink in center and juices run clear, turning once. Brush with sauce during the last 10 minutes of grilling. If desired, garnish with plum wedges. Makes 4 servings.

Nutrition information per serving: 224 calories, 20 g protein, 11 g carbohydrate, 11 g fat (4 g saturated fat), 66 mg cholesterol, 283 mg sodium.

Spicy Fruit and Pork Kabobs

Tangy pineapple and cool cantaloupe complement the spicy flavor of this pork on a stick.

1½	pounds lean boneless pork
2	tablespoons olive oil or cooking oil
2	tablespoons balsamic vinegar
1	teaspoon finely shredded orange peel
2	tablespoons orange juice
1	clove garlic, minced
¼	teaspoon salt
¼	teaspoon ground cumin
12	1½-inch cubes fresh pineapple
12	1½-inch cubes cantaloupe

Trim fat from meat. Cut into 1½-inch cubes. Place meat in a plastic bag and set bag into a shallow dish. For marinade, combine oil, balsamic vinegar, orange peel, orange juice, garlic, salt, and cumin. Pour over meat; seal bag.

Marinate in the refrigerator for 2 to 4 hours, turning bag once. Drain meat, reserving marinade. Alternately thread meat, pineapple, and cantaloupe onto 6 long metal skewers.

Grill kabobs on an uncovered grill directly over medium coals for 14 to 16 minutes or until meat is slightly pink in center and juices run clear, turning and brushing once with marinade halfway through grilling. Makes 6 servings.

Nutrition information per serving: 181 calories, 16 g protein, 6 g carbohydrate, 10 g fat (3 g saturated fat), 51 mg cholesterol, 87 mg sodium.

Pork Medallions with Cherry Sauce

During the autumn months, pork is often prepared with fruit such as prunes or apples. These quick-seared medallions cloaked in a delightful sweet cherry sauce provide a whole new reason—and season—to pair pork with fruit.

1 pound pork tenderloin
Nonstick spray coating
¾ cup cranberry juice or apple juice
2 teaspoons spicy brown mustard
1 teaspoon cornstarch
1 cup sweet cherries (such as Rainier or Bing), halved and pitted, or 1 cup frozen unsweetened pitted dark sweet cherries, thawed

Trim fat from meat. Cut meat crosswise into 1-inch-thick slices. Place each slice between two pieces of plastic wrap. With the heel of your hand, press each slice into a ½-inch-thick medallion. Remove plastic wrap. Sprinkle meat lightly with salt and pepper.

Spray an unheated large nonstick skillet with nonstick coating. Heat skillet over medium-high heat. Add meat and cook for 4 to 6 minutes or until meat is slightly pink in center and juices run clear, turning once. Remove from skillet; keep warm.

Combine the cranberry or apple juice, mustard, and cornstarch; add to skillet. Cook and stir until thickened and bubbly. Cook and stir for 2 minutes more. Stir cherries into cranberry mixture. Serve over meat. Makes 4 servings.

Nutrition information per serving: 197 calories, 26 g protein, 12 g carbohydrate, 5 g fat (2 g saturated fat), 81 mg cholesterol, 127 mg sodium.

FREEZING CHERRIES

Enjoy Pork Medallions with Cherry Sauce (above) year round by freezing your own supply of summer cherries. Rinse, dry, and pit the cherries. Place cherries in freezer bags or freezer containers, leaving ½-inch headspace. Freeze the cherries for 6 to 12 months. To thaw the cherries, set out at room temperature about 30 minutes.

Mustard-Orange Pork Tenderloin

A mixture of vegetables, such as cut-up red onions, baby carrots, and chunks of zucchini, can be roasted alongside the meat. Just spray the vegetables with olive oil-flavored nonstick spray coating before placing them in the pan around the meat.

12 ounces pork tenderloin
½ cup apricot preserves or orange marmalade
3 tablespoons Dijon-style mustard
Nonstick spray coating
2 cups sliced fresh mushrooms
½ cup sliced green onions
2 tablespoons orange juice

Trim fat from meat. Place meat on a rack in a shallow roasting pan. Insert a meat thermometer into the center of meat. Roast, uncovered, in a 425° oven for 10 minutes.

Meanwhile, in a small bowl stir together preserves or marmalade and mustard. Spoon half of the mustard mixture over the meat. Set the remaining mustard mixture aside.

Roast for 15 to 25 minutes more or until the meat thermometer registers 155°. Transfer the meat to a warm platter and cover with foil. Let stand for 10 minutes before slicing. (The meat's temperature will rise 5° during standing.)

Meanwhile, spray a medium saucepan with nonstick coating. Add mushrooms and green onions. Cook and stir for 2 to 3 minutes or until mushrooms are tender. Stir in the remaining mustard mixture and orange juice. Cook and stir until heated through.

To serve, thinly slice the meat. Spoon the mushroom mixture over meat. Makes 4 servings.

Nutrition information per serving: 240 calories, 21 g protein, 32 g carbohydrate, 4 g fat (1 g saturated), 60 mg cholesterol, 334 mg sodium.

Cashew Pork and Broccoli

The Portuguese brought the cashew from the New World to India and East Africa in the fifteenth century. From there it traveled to China and worked its way into Chinese cuisine.

12 ounces lean boneless pork
2 tablespoons soy sauce
2 teaspoons toasted sesame oil
2 teaspoons grated gingerroot
2 cloves garlic, minced
½ cup hoisin sauce
½ cup water
2 tablespoons soy sauce
1 tablespoon cornstarch
1 teaspoon sugar
⅛ teaspoon crushed red pepper
1 tablespoon cooking oil
2 medium onions, cut into thin
    wedges
2 stalks celery, thinly bias-sliced
3 cups broccoli flowerets
2 cups hot cooked rice
½ cup dry roasted cashews

Trim fat from meat. Partially freeze the meat. Thinly slice across the grain into bite-size strips. In a medium bowl combine the meat strips, 2 tablespoons soy sauce, sesame oil, gingerroot, and garlic. Cover and chill for 1 to 2 hours.

For sauce, in a small mixing bowl stir together the hoisin sauce, water, 2 tablespoons soy sauce, cornstarch, sugar, and crushed red pepper. Set aside.

Add cooking oil to a wok or large skillet. Preheat over medium-high heat (add more oil if necessary during cooking.) Stir-fry onions and celery in hot oil for 1 minute. Add broccoli; stir-fry for 3 to 4 minutes or until crisp-tender. Remove vegetables from wok.

Add meat mixture to wok. Stir-fry for 2 to 3 minutes or until meat is slightly pink in center. Push meat from center of wok.

Stir sauce; add to center of wok. Cook and stir until thickened and bubbly. Return cooked vegetables to wok. Stir all ingredients together to coat. Cover and cook about 1 minute more or until heated through. Serve immediately with hot cooked rice. Sprinkle with cashews. Makes 4 servings.

Nutrition information per serving: 480 calories, 21 g protein, 42 g carbohydrate, 26 g fat (5 g saturated fat), 38 mg cholesterol, 1,554 mg sodium.

Down-Home Ribs

Down-Home Ribs

Fresh gingerroot adds an enticing bite to the sauce. Store extra gingerroot in an air-tight container in your freezer and then just grate as needed.

1	medium onion, chopped
1	tablespoon cooking oil
⅓	cup catsup
2	tablespoons orange juice
1	tablespoon brown sugar
1	teaspoon chili powder
½	teaspoon grated gingerroot
4	pounds pork loin back ribs or meaty spareribs

For sauce, in a medium skillet cook onion in hot oil over medium heat about 4 minutes or until onion is tender. Stir in catsup, orange juice, brown sugar, chili powder, and gingerroot. Cook about 5 minutes more or until sauce is slightly thickened. Remove from heat. Trim fat from ribs. Cut ribs into serving-size pieces.

In a covered grill arrange medium-hot coals around a drip pan. Test for medium heat above the pan. Place the ribs on grill rack over drip pan. Cover and grill for 1¼ to 1½ hours or until ribs are tender. Brush occasionally with sauce during the last 10 minutes of grilling. Makes 6 servings.

Nutrition information per serving: 313 calories, 19 g protein, 8 g carbohydrate, 22 g fat (8 g saturated), 79 mg cholesterol, 245 mg sodium.

Sweet and Tangy Country-Style Ribs

Serve this summertime classic with other picnic favorites, such as corn on the cob and coleslaw.

½	cup chili sauce
2	tablespoons apple jelly
1	tablespoon vinegar
1	teaspoon prepared mustard
1	teaspoon Worcestershire sauce
¼	teaspoon chili powder
2	to 2½ pounds pork country-style ribs

For sauce, in a small saucepan cook and stir chili sauce and jelly until jelly is melted. Stir in vinegar, mustard, Worcestershire sauce, and chili powder. Remove from heat. Trim fat from ribs.

In a covered grill arrange medium-hot coals around a drip pan. Test for medium heat above the pan. Place ribs on grill rack over drip pan. Cover and grill for 1½ to 2 hours or until ribs are tender. Brush occasionally with sauce during the last 15 minutes of grilling. Serve with any remaining sauce. Makes 4 servings.

Nutrition information per serving: 449 calories, 33 g protein, 15 g carbohydrate, 28 g fat (10 g saturated), 129 mg cholesterol, 533 mg sodium.

Ham, Spinach, and Mostaccioli Casserole

Just before serving, be sure to give the casserole a good stir to distribute the rich and creamy sauce.

8	ounces packaged dried mostaccioli, cut ziti, or elbow macaroni
3	tablespoons margarine or butter
3	medium onions, cut into thin wedges, or 5 medium leeks, sliced
2	cloves garlic, minced
¼	cup all-purpose flour
½	teaspoon dried thyme, crushed
⅛	teaspoon pepper
1½	cups half-and-half, light cream, or milk
1½	cups chicken broth
1½	cups cubed fully cooked ham
1	10-ounce package frozen chopped spinach, thawed and drained

Cook pasta according to package directions. Drain pasta; rinse with cold water. Drain again.

In a large saucepan melt margarine or butter. Add onions or leeks and garlic. Cover and cook about 5 minutes or until onions are tender, stirring occasionally. Stir in flour, thyme, and pepper. Add half-and-half, light cream, or milk and the chicken broth all at once. Cook and stir until thickened and bubbly. Cook and stir for 1 minute more. Stir in pasta, ham, and spinach. Spoon mixture into a 3-quart casserole.

Cover and bake in a 350° oven for 30 to 35 minutes or until heated through. Let stand for 5 minutes. Stir gently before serving. Makes 6 servings.

Nutrition information per serving: 388 calories, 18 g protein, 44 g carbohydrate, 16 g fat (6 g saturated), 42 mg cholesterol, 719 mg sodium.

Thawing Spinach

When you forget to thaw frozen spinach ahead of time, place the unwrapped frozen block of spinach in a colander and run hot water over it, breaking up the block with a fork. If you prefer, you can micro-thaw spinach by placing the unwrapped block in a bowl and micro-cooking it on 30% power (medium-low) for 2 to 4 minutes or until soft enough to break into chunks. Continue to cook the spinach on 30% power for 3 to 5 minutes or until thawed.

Italian Pizza Sandwiches

Some like it hot! If you do, choose the hot sausage. For those with less adventurous palates, choose the mild or sweet sausage. You may want to grill some of each.

1　medium green sweet pepper, cut into thin strips
1　medium onion, thinly sliced
1　tablespoon margarine or butter
4　uncooked mild or hot Italian sausage links (12 to 16 ounces total)
½　cup pizza sauce
4　individual French-style rolls, split
2　tablespoons grated Parmesan cheese

Fold a 36x18-inch piece of heavy foil in half to make an 18-inch square. Place green pepper and onion in the center of the foil. Dot with margarine or butter.

Bring up two opposite edges of foil and seal with a double fold. Then fold remaining ends to completely enclose vegetables, leaving space for steam to build. Prick the sausage links in several places with a fork or the tip of a sharp knife.

In a covered grill arrange medium-hot coals around a drip pan. Test for medium heat above the pan. Place sausage links and vegetable packet on grill rack over drip pan. Cover and grill for 20 to 25 minutes or until sausage juices run clear and vegetables are tender.

Meanwhile, in a small saucepan heat pizza sauce. Toast cut sides of French rolls on grill.

To serve, halve the sausage links lengthwise, cutting to, but not through, the other side. Place sausage links in the toasted rolls. Top with the grilled vegetables and warm pizza sauce. Sprinkle with Parmesan cheese. Makes 4 servings.

Nutrition information per serving: 376 calories, 18 g protein, 26 g carbohydrate, 22 g fat (7 g saturated), 51 mg cholesterol, 1,067 mg sodium.

Bow Ties with Sausage & Peppers

You will be amazed that so few ingredients generate so much flavor. To reduce the fat, use Italian-style ground turkey sausage.

8 ounces packaged dried large bow-tie pasta	Cook pasta according to package directions. Drain; keep warm. Meanwhile, cut the sausage into 1-inch pieces. In a large skillet cook sausage and sweet peppers over medium-high heat until sausage is brown. Drain fat.
12 ounces spicy Italian sausage links	
2 medium red sweet peppers, cut into ¾-inch pieces	
½ cup vegetable broth or beef broth	Stir the vegetable or beef broth and black pepper into sausage mixture. Bring to boiling; reduce heat. Simmer, uncovered, for 5 minutes. Remove from heat. Pour the sausage mixture over pasta; add parsley. Toss gently to coat. Makes 4 servings.
¼ teaspoon coarsely ground black pepper	
¼ cup snipped Italian flat-leaf parsley	

Nutrition information per serving: 397 calories, 24 g protein, 38 g carbohydrate, 18 g fat (6 g saturated), 94 mg cholesterol, 713 mg sodium.

Greek-Style Pasta Skillet

Lamb, cinnamon, and feta cheese add a Greek twist to this macaroni casserole.

12 ounces ground lamb or lean ground beef	In a large skillet cook ground meat and onion until meat is brown. Drain fat. Stir in the undrained tomatoes, tomato juice, water, bouillon granules, cinnamon, and garlic powder.
1 medium onion, chopped (½ cup)	
1 14½-ounce can diced tomatoes	
1 5½-ounce can tomato juice	Bring to boiling. Stir the uncooked pasta and green beans into meat mixture. Return to boiling; reduce heat. Cover and simmer about 15 minutes or until pasta and green beans are tender. Sprinkle with feta cheese. Makes 4 servings.
½ cup water	
½ teaspoon instant beef bouillon granules	
½ teaspoon ground cinnamon	
⅛ teaspoon garlic powder	
1 cup packaged dried medium shell macaroni or elbow macaroni	
1 cup loose-pack frozen cut green beans	
½ cup crumbled feta cheese	

Nutrition information per serving: 362 calories, 22 g protein, 33 g carbohydrate, 16 g fat (7 g saturated fat), 70 mg cholesterol, 647 mg sodium.

Greek-Style Pasta Skillet

Grecian Kabobs

Take your pick ... lamb or pork. Both meats are equally delicious when speared on these herb-scented kabobs.

1 pound lean boneless lamb or pork
2 tablespoons olive oil or cooking oil
2 tablespoons lemon juice
1 tablespoon snipped fresh chives or
   1 teaspoon dried chives
1 tablespoon snipped fresh oregano or
   1 teaspoon dried oregano, crushed
1 tablespoon water
1 clove garlic, minced
1 medium red onion, cut into wedges
1 medium green sweet pepper, cut
   into 1-inch squares
2 cups fresh mushrooms
   Hot cooked couscous (optional)*
   Fresh oregano sprigs (optional)

Trim fat from meat. Cut meat into 1-inch cubes. Place meat in a plastic bag and set the bag into a shallow dish. For marinade, in a small bowl combine olive or cooking oil, lemon juice, chives, snipped fresh or dried oregano, water, and garlic. Pour over meat; seal bag. Marinate in the refrigerator for 4 to 24 hours, turning the bag occasionally.

Meanwhile, cook onion wedges in a small amount of boiling water for 3 minutes. Drain and cool slightly.

Drain meat, reserving marinade. On 8 short or 4 long metal skewers, alternately thread meat cubes, onion, green pepper, and mushrooms, leaving about ¼ inch space between pieces.

Grill the kabobs on an uncovered grill directly over medium coals for 12 to 14 minutes or until meat is slightly pink in center, turning and brushing once with marinade halfway through grilling.

(Or, in a covered grill arrange medium-hot coals around a drip pan. Test for medium heat above pan. Place kabobs on grill rack over drip pan. Cover and grill for 16 to 18 minutes, brushing once with marinade halfway through grilling)

If desired, serve over hot cooked couscous and garnish with fresh oregano sprigs. Makes 4 servings.

*Note: If you like, stir 1 small tomato, chopped, and 2 green onions, thinly sliced, into the boiling water with the couscous.

Nutrition information per serving: 177 calories, 19 g protein, 5 g carbohydrate, 9 g fat (3 g saturated), 57 mg cholesterol, 46 mg sodium.

Poultry

Contents

KEYS-STYLE CITRUS CHICKEN
(recipe, page 114)

Ruby-Glazed Chicken Breasts

These chicken breasts have such a rich flavor from the currant and apple glaze that you would never guess they are low in fat—only 3 grams per serving.

⅓ cup apple juice
3 tablespoons currant jelly
1 teaspoon cornstarch
¼ teaspoon salt
⅛ teaspoon dried marjoram, crushed
3 whole small chicken breasts
   (about 2¼ pounds total),
   halved lengthwise

For sauce, in a small saucepan combine apple juice, currant jelly, cornstarch, and salt. Cook and stir over medium heat until thickened and bubbly. Cook and stir for 2 minutes more. Remove from heat. Stir in the marjoram. Set aside.

If desired, skin chicken. Rinse chicken; pat dry with paper towels.

Grill chicken, bone side up, on an uncovered grill directly over medium coals for 35 to 45 minutes or until chicken is tender and no longer pink, turning and brushing once with sauce.

(Or, in a covered grill arrange medium-hot coals around a drip pan. Test for medium heat above the pan. Place chicken, bone side down, on grill rack over drip pan. Cover and grill for 50 to 60 minutes. Brush occasionally with sauce during the last 20 minutes of grilling.)

Brush the grilled chicken with any remaining sauce before serving. Makes 6 servings.

Nutrition information per serving: 167 calories, 25 g protein, 9 g carbohydrate, 3 g fat (1 g saturated), 69 mg cholesterol, 150 mg sodium.

Southwest Chicken Breasts

To transform this dish into a salad, slice the chicken breasts and arrange them on plates lined with shredded lettuce. Top with the avocado mixture for a chunky dressing and add some shredded Monterey Jack cheese.

6 medium skinless, boneless chicken breast halves (about 1½ pounds total)

¼ cup dry white wine

2 tablespoons olive oil or cooking oil

2 teaspoons snipped fresh tarragon or ¼ teaspoon dried tarragon, crushed

¼ teaspoon salt

2 avocados, seeded, peeled, and chopped

1 tomato, chopped

2 green onions, finely chopped

2 tablespoons finely chopped, seeded green chile peppers (such as jalapeño, serrano, or Anaheim)

1 tablespoon snipped cilantro

1 tablespoon honey

1 tablespoon lemon juice

1 clove garlic, minced

Lettuce leaves (optional)

Rinse chicken; pat dry with paper towels. Place chicken in a plastic bag and set the bag into a shallow dish. For marinade, in a small bowl combine the white wine, oil, tarragon, and salt. Pour over chicken; seal bag. Marinate in the refrigerator for 2 to 24 hours, turning bag occasionally.

Meanwhile, combine avocados, tomato, green onions, chile peppers, cilantro, honey, lemon juice, and garlic. Toss gently to mix. Cover and chill up to 2 hours.

Drain chicken, reserving marinade. Grill chicken on an uncovered grill directly over medium coals for 12 to 15 minutes or until tender and no longer pink, turning and brushing once with marinade halfway through grilling.

(Or, in a covered grill arrange medium-hot coals around a drip pan. Test for medium heat above the pan. Place chicken on grill rack over drip pan. Cover and grill for 15 to 18 minutes. Brush occasionally with marinade up to the last 5 minutes of grilling.)

Serve the grilled chicken with avocado mixture and, if desired, lettuce leaves. Makes 6 servings.

Nutrition information per serving: 239 calories, 20 g protein, 5 g carbohydrate, 16 g fat (1 g saturated), 50 mg cholesterol, 130 mg sodium.

Keys-Style Citrus Chicken

The tropical-island-inspired cooking of the Florida Keys draws on the best of both worlds. Here, it combines fresh Florida citrus with the Caribbean penchant for fiery peppers. Soak up the delicious juice with hot cooked rice.

4 medium skinless, boneless chicken breast halves (about 1 pound total)
2 or 3 cloves garlic, peeled and thinly sliced
1 tablespoon butter or margarine
1 teaspoon finely shredded lime peel
2 tablespoons lime juice
¼ teaspoon ground ginger
⅛ teaspoon crushed red pepper
1 orange
   Hot cooked rice (optional)
   Lime wedges (optional)

Rinse chicken; pat dry with paper towels. In a large skillet cook chicken and garlic in butter or margarine over medium heat for 8 to 10 minutes or until chicken is tender and no longer pink, turning chicken once and stirring garlic occasionally.

Meanwhile, in a small bowl combine lime peel, lime juice, ginger, and red pepper; set aside. Peel orange. Reserving juice, cut orange in half lengthwise, then cut crosswise into slices. Add any reserved orange juice and the lime juice mixture to skillet.

Place the orange slices on top of chicken. Cover and cook for 1 to 2 minutes more or until heated through.

To serve, spoon any reserved drippings over chicken. If desired, serve with cooked rice and garnish with lime wedges. Makes 4 servings.

Nutrition information per serving: 167 calories, 22 g protein, 5 g carbohydrate, 6 g fat (3 g saturated), 67 mg cholesterol, 84 mg sodium.

Chicken with Peas and Potatoes

Save clean-up time with this chicken meal-in-a-skillet featuring tiny potatoes and peas in a rosemary-scented sauce.

1	2½- to 3 pound cut up broiler fryer chicken or 2 pounds chicken thighs
1	pound small new potatoes, quartered
2	tablespoons margarine or butter
¾	cup chicken broth
1	teaspoon dried rosemary, crushed
¼	teaspoon pepper
4	green onions, thinly sliced
1	10-ounce package frozen peas
¼	cup snipped parsley
1	8-ounce carton dairy sour cream
2	tablespoons all-purpose flour

Skin chicken, if desired. Rinse and pat dry with paper towels. Scrub the potatoes.

In a 12-inch skillet cook chicken in hot margarine or butter over medium heat about 15 minutes or until chicken is browned, turning to brown evenly. Add potatoes, broth, rosemary, and pepper. Bring to boiling; reduce heat. Cover and simmer for 30 minutes.

Add green onion, peas, and ¼ cup parsley to skillet. Cover and simmer about 10 minutes more or until the chicken and potatoes are tender and chicken is no longer pink. Using a slotted spoon, transfer chicken and vegetables to a platter; keep warm.

Remove skillet from heat. Stir together sour cream and flour; stir into broth in skillet. Cook and stir until thickened and bubbly; cook and stir for 1 minute more. Spoon sauce over chicken and vegetables. Makes 6 servings.

Nutrition information per serving: 491 calories, 34 g protein, 28 g carbohydrate, 27 g fat (10 g saturated), 106 mg cholesterol, 286 mg sodium

Honeyed Chicken

For a zippy appetizer, use this glaze for 10 to 12 chicken wings (cut the wings at the joints and discard tips).

8	chicken drumsticks and/or thighs (about 2 pounds total)
¼	cup finely chopped green onions
¼	cup honey
¼	teaspoon garlic powder
	Dash ground red pepper

Arrange washed chicken in a 15x10x1-inch baking pan so the pieces don't touch. Bake in a 400° oven for 30 minutes.

Meanwhile, combine the chopped green onions, honey, garlic powder, and ground red pepper. Brush over chicken. Bake for 15 to 20 minutes more or until chicken is tender and no longer pink. Makes 4 servings.

Nutrition information per serving: 327 calories, 29 g protein, 17 g carbohydrate, 15 g fat (4 g saturated), 103 mg cholesterol, 98 mg sodium.

Chicken and Vegetable Skillet

Try this combination another time with angel hair pasta and a sprinkle of freshly grated Parmesan cheese.

1	2½- to 3-pound broiler-fryer chicken, cut up
¼	cup all-purpose flour
½	teaspoon salt
½	teaspoon paprika
¼	teaspoon pepper
2	tablespoons cooking oil
½	cup chopped onion
2	cloves garlic, minced
1	tablespoon grated gingerroot
¾	cup chicken broth
1	pound fresh asparagus, cut into 1-inch pieces
3	yellow summer squash and/or zucchini, cut into 1-inch chunks
8	ounces fresh mushrooms, thickly sliced (3 cups)
2	red or green sweet peppers, cut into 1-inch strips
¼	cup dry sherry
2	tablespoons soy sauce
2	teaspoons cornstarch
	Hot cooked orzo, rice, or noodles

If desired, skin chicken. Rinse chicken; pat dry with paper towels. In a plastic or paper bag combine flour, salt, paprika, and pepper. Add chicken, a few pieces at a time, shaking to coat well.

In a 12-inch skillet cook the chicken pieces in hot oil over medium heat about 10 minutes or until lightly browned, turning to brown evenly. Remove the chicken. If necessary, add 1 tablespoon additional oil to skillet.

Add the chopped onion, garlic, and gingerroot to skillet. Cook for 4 to 5 minutes or until onion is tender. Carefully stir in chicken broth. Return chicken to skillet.

Bring to boiling; reduce heat. Cover and simmer about 15 minutes or until chicken is tender and no longer pink. Spoon off fat.

Add asparagus, squash, mushrooms, and sweet peppers. In a measuring cup combine the dry sherry, soy sauce, and cornstarch; stir into chicken mixture.

Return to boiling; reduce heat. Cover and simmer for 5 to 10 minutes more or until vegetables are crisp-tender. Serve with cooked orzo, rice, or noodles. Makes 4 to 6 servings.

Nutrition information per serving: 621 calories, 51 g protein, 33 g carbohydrate, 31 g fat (7 g saturated), 134 mg cholesterol, 1,069 mg sodium.

Chicken with Apricots and Prunes

Boost the flavor in the rice accompaniment with toasted slivered almonds and snipped parsley.

2 to 2½ pounds meaty chicken pieces
 (breasts, thighs, and drumsticks)
½ teaspoon salt
½ teaspoon garlic powder
¼ teaspoon pepper
2 tablespoons cooking oil
1 6-ounce package dried apricots
1 cup pitted prunes, cut into halves
1 cup chicken broth
¾ cup dry white wine
¼ cup white wine vinegar
1 tablespoon brown sugar
3 inches stick cinnamon
4 whole cloves
3 tablespoons Dijon-style mustard
3 tablespoons water
4 teaspoons all-purpose flour
 Hot cooked rice
 Thinly sliced green onion (optional)

If desired, skin chicken. Rinse chicken; pat dry with paper towels. Sprinkle chicken with salt, garlic powder, and pepper.

In a 4½-quart Dutch oven cook chicken in hot cooking oil over medium heat about 15 minutes or until lightly browned, turning to brown evenly. Drain fat.

Add apricots, prunes, chicken broth, white wine, wine vinegar, brown sugar, cinnamon, and cloves. Bring to boiling; reduce heat. Cover and simmer for 35 to 40 minutes or until chicken is tender and no longer pink.

Using a slotted spoon, transfer the chicken and fruit to a serving platter; keep warm. Discard cinnamon and cloves. For sauce, in a small bowl stir together the Dijon mustard, water, and flour. Stir into the broth mixture. Cook and stir until thickened and bubbly. Cook and stir for 1 minute more.

Serve chicken and fruit over cooked rice. Top with some of the sauce. If desired, garnish with sliced green onion. Pass the remaining sauce. Makes 6 servings.

Nutrition information per serving: 570 calories, 29 g protein, 82 g carbohydrate, 13 g fat (3 g saturated), 69 mg cholesterol, 580 mg sodium.

Texas-Style Barbecued Chicken Legs

Cut lengthwise strips of assorted sweet peppers and grill to perfection alongside the chicken.

1   medium onion, finely chopped
        (½ cup)
2   cloves garlic, minced
1   teaspoon chili powder
¼   teaspoon ground sage
1   tablespoon margarine or butter
½   cup catsup
2   tablespoons water
2   tablespoons vinegar
1   tablespoon sugar
1   tablespoon lemon juice
1   tablespoon Worcestershire sauce
½   teaspoon salt
½   teaspoon bottled hot pepper sauce
¼   teaspoon cracked black pepper
6   chicken legs (thigh-drumstick
        pieces) (3 to 3½ pounds total)

For sauce, in a small saucepan cook onion, garlic, chili powder, and sage in margarine or butter until onion is tender. Stir in catsup, water, vinegar, sugar, lemon juice, Worcestershire sauce, salt, hot pepper sauce, and black pepper. Bring to boiling; reduce heat. Simmer, uncovered, for 5 minutes, stirring occasionally.

Meanwhile, rinse chicken; pat dry with paper towels. Grill chicken, skin side down, on an uncovered grill directly over medium coals for 35 to 40 minutes or until chicken is tender and no longer pink, turning once. (Or, place chicken on the unheated rack of a broiler pan. Broil 5 to 6 inches from the heat for 28 to 32 minutes, turning once.) Brush with sauce during the last 10 minutes of grilling or broiling.

Heat the remaining sauce until bubbly. Pass the sauce with chicken. Makes 6 servings.

Nutrition information per serving: 276 calories, 25 g protein, 11 g carbohydrate, 15 g fat (4 g saturated), 86 mg cholesterol, 596 mg sodium.

𝒯EST THE TEMPERATURE

Before you grill, check the temperature of the coals. Hold your hand, palm side down, in the location you plan to place the food. Count "one thousand one, one thousand two," etc., for as long as you can hold your hand there. Two seconds means the coals are hot, three is medium-hot, four is medium, five is medium-slow, and six is slow.

Curried Chicken Thighs

You also can use skinless, boneless chicken thighs in this Indian-style recipe. Just reduce the cooking time to 10 minutes after adding the chicken broth.

8 chicken thighs (about 2½ pounds total)
2 tablespoons cooking oil
1 cup sliced fresh mushrooms
1 medium onion, chopped (½ cup)
1 clove garlic, minced
3 to 4 teaspoons curry powder
¼ teaspoon salt
¼ teaspoon ground cinnamon
¾ cup chicken broth
1 medium apple, cored and chopped
1 cup half-and-half, light cream, or milk
2 tablespoons all-purpose flour
3 cups hot cooked rice
   Assorted condiments: raisins, chopped hard-cooked egg, peanuts, chopped tomato, chopped green sweet pepper, toasted coconut, chutney, cut-up fruits (optional)

Skin chicken. Rinse chicken; pat dry with paper towels. In a 10-inch skillet cook chicken in hot oil over medium heat about 10 minutes or until lightly browned, turning to brown evenly. Remove chicken. If necessary, add 1 tablespoon additional cooking oil to skillet.

Add mushrooms, onion, and garlic to skillet; cook until vegetables are tender. Add curry powder, salt, and cinnamon; cook and stir for 1 minute. Add chicken broth and apple. Return chicken to skillet. Bring to boiling; reduce heat. Cover and simmer about 15 minutes or until chicken is tender and no longer pink.

Transfer chicken to platter; keep warm. Stir the half-and-half, light cream, or milk into the flour. Stir into pan juices. Cook and stir until thickened and bubbly. Cook and stir for 1 minute more. Spoon some sauce over chicken. Pass remaining sauce. Serve with rice and, if desired, pass condiments. Makes 4 servings.

Nutrition information per serving: 695 calories, 54 g protein, 45 g carbohydrate, 32 g fat (10 g saturated), 158 mg cholesterol, 829 mg sodium.

Minnesota Apple- and Wild Rice-Stuffed Chicken

Team up this bird with a chicory and red onion salad dressed with a blue cheese vinaigrette.

1 6-ounce package long grain and wild rice mix
8 ounces sliced fresh mushrooms (3 cups)
2 medium cooking apples (such as Granny Smith or Jonathan), cored and chopped
1 cup shredded carrot
½ cup thinly sliced green onions
½ teaspoon pepper
1 5- to 6-pound whole roasting chicken
2 to 3 tablespoons apple jelly, melted
Apple wedges (optional)

For stuffing, cook rice according to package directions, except add mushrooms, apples, shredded carrot, green onions, and pepper to rice before cooking.

Meanwhile, rinse chicken; pat dry with paper towels. Spoon some of the stuffing loosely into the neck cavity. Pull neck skin to back; fasten with a small skewer. Lightly spoon the remaining stuffing into the body cavity. Tuck the drumsticks under the band of skin that crosses the tail. If there is no band, tie the drumsticks to tail. Twist the wing tips under the chicken.

Place stuffed chicken, breast side up, on a rack in a shallow roasting pan. Insert meat thermometer into the center of an inside thigh muscle. The bulb should not touch the bone.

Roast, uncovered, in a 325° oven for 1¾ to 2½ hours or until meat thermometer registers 180°. At this time, chicken is no longer pink and the drumsticks move easily in their sockets. When the bird is two-thirds done, cut the band of skin or string between drumsticks so thighs will cook evenly. Brush chicken with melted jelly once or twice during the last 10 minutes of roasting.

Remove the chicken from oven; cover with foil. Let stand for 10 to 20 minutes before carving. Transfer chicken to a serving platter. Spoon some of the stuffing around the chicken. If desired, garnish with apple wedges. Pass the remaining stuffing. Makes 10 servings.

Nutrition information per serving: 332 calories, 34 g protein, 19 g carbohydrate, 13 g fat (4 g saturated), 93 mg cholesterol, 365 mg sodium.

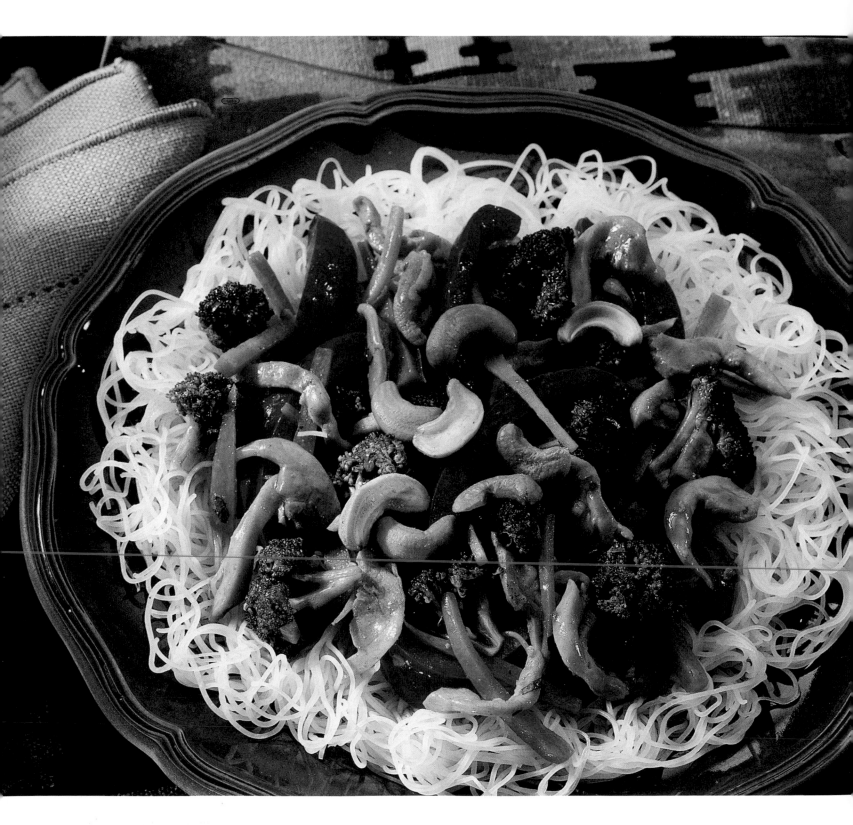

Pacific Rim Stir-Fry

Adjust the hotness of this stir-fry by reducing or increasing the amount of chile oil used.

3 ounces rice sticks (also called rice noodles) or packaged dried vermicelli, broken

12 ounces skinless, boneless chicken thighs or breast halves

½ cup chicken broth

2 tablespoons snipped fresh basil or 2 teaspoons dried basil, crushed

2 tablespoons soy sauce

2 teaspoons cornstarch

1 teaspoon chile oil or ½ teaspoon crushed red pepper

½ teaspoon ground turmeric

1 tablespoon cooking oil

2 medium carrots, cut into julienne strips

2 cups broccoli flowerets

1 red or green sweet pepper, cut into lengthwise strips

¼ cup cashew halves or peanuts

In a saucepan cook rice sticks in boiling water for 3 minutes. (Or, cook vermicelli according to package directions.) Drain; keep warm.

Meanwhile, rinse chicken; pat dry with paper towels. Cut chicken thighs or breasts into thin, bite-size strips; set aside.

For sauce, in a small bowl combine chicken broth, basil, soy sauce, cornstarch, chile oil or crushed red pepper, and turmeric; set aside.

Add cooking oil to a wok or 12-inch skillet. Preheat over medium-high heat (add more oil if necessary during cooking). Stir-fry carrot strips in hot oil for 1 minute. Add broccoli; stir-fry for 2 minutes. Add sweet pepper strips; stir-fry for 1½ to 3 minutes more or until crisp-tender. Remove from wok. Add the chicken to wok; stir-fry for 2 to 3 minutes or until tender and no longer pink. Push from center of wok.

Stir sauce; add to center of wok. Cook and stir until thickened and bubbly. Return cooked vegetables to wok. Stir all ingredients together to coat. Cook and stir about 2 minutes more or until heated through. Serve immediately over hot rice sticks or vermicelli. Top with cashews or peanuts. Makes 4 servings.

Nutrition information per serving: 309 calories, 17 g protein, 32 g carbohydrate, 13 g fat (3 g saturated), 41 mg cholesterol, 748 mg sodium.

Chicken and Apple Stir-Fry

This sweet-spiced dish includes an array of colorful peppers, plus dried mushrooms, crunchy almonds, and crisp, tart apple slices.

6 dried mushrooms (such as shiitake or wood ear mushrooms)

12 ounces skinless, boneless chicken breast halves or turkey breast tenderloin steaks

¾ cup cold water

3 tablespoons frozen orange, apple, or pineapple juice concentrate, thawed

2 tablespoons soy sauce

2 teaspoons cornstarch

¼ teaspoon ground ginger

¼ teaspoon ground cinnamon

⅛ to ¼ teaspoon ground red pepper

¼ cup sliced or slivered almonds

1 tablespoon cooking oil

2 medium green, red, orange, and/or yellow sweet peppers, cut into thin strips

2 medium apples, thinly sliced

2 cups hot cooked brown rice

In a small bowl cover mushrooms with warm water. Let soak for 30 minutes. Rinse and squeeze the mushrooms to drain thoroughly. Discard stems. Thinly slice mushrooms. Set aside.

Meanwhile, rinse chicken or turkey; pat dry with paper towels. Cut into 1-inch pieces. Set aside.

For sauce, in a small mixing bowl stir together the cold water, juice concentrate, soy sauce, cornstarch, ginger, cinnamon, and ground red pepper. Set aside.

Preheat a wok or large skillet over medium-high heat. Add almonds; stir-fry for 2 to 3 minutes or until golden. Remove almonds from wok. Let wok cool slightly.

Add cooking oil to wok. Preheat over medium-high heat (add more oil if necessary during cooking). Stir-fry mushrooms, sweet peppers, and apples in hot oil for 1 to 2 minutes or until peppers and apples are crisp-tender. Remove apple mixture from wok.

Add chicken to wok. Stir-fry for 3 to 4 minutes or until tender and no longer pink. Push chicken from center of wok. Stir sauce; add to center of wok. Cook and stir until thickened and bubbly. Return apple mixture to wok. Stir all ingredients together to coat. Cook and stir for 1 to 2 minutes more or until heated through.

Stir in toasted almonds. Serve immediately over hot cooked brown rice. Makes 4 servings.

Nutrition information per serving: 370 calories, 22 g protein, 48 g carbohydrate, 11 g fat (2 g saturated fat), 45 mg cholesterol, 563 mg sodium.

Quick Chicken Fajitas

For a delicious one-dish meal, begin with chicken and a few simple ingredients. Round out dinner with scoops of your favorite ice cream or sherbet and raspberries or sliced strawberries.

8	7-inch flour tortillas
12	ounces skinless, boneless chicken breast halves or turkey breast tenderloin steaks
1	tablespoon lime juice or lemon juice
½	teaspoon ground cumin
½	teaspoon ground coriander
¼	teaspoon dried oregano, crushed
¼	cup clear Italian salad dressing (not reduced-fat dressing)
¾	cup red and/or green sweet pepper cut into strips
1	small onion, halved lengthwise and sliced
	Assorted condiments: salsa, dairy sour cream, guacamole, jalapeño peppers
	Shredded lettuce (optional)

Wrap tortillas in foil. Heat in a 350° oven for 10 to 15 minutes or until heated through. Or, wrap in paper towels or waxed paper and heat in a microwave oven on 100% power (high) for 15 to 20 seconds.

Meanwhile, rinse chicken or turkey; pat dry with paper towels. Thinly slice chicken or turkey into bite-size strips. In a medium bowl combine lime or lemon juice, cumin, coriander, and oregano. Stir in chicken or turkey; set aside.

In a large skillet heat the salad dressing over medium-high heat. Add chicken mixture. Cook and stir about 2 minutes or until chicken is tender and no longer pink. With a slotted spoon, remove the chicken from skillet.

Add sweet pepper and sliced onion to skillet; cook and stir for 2 to 3 minutes or until vegetables are crisp-tender. Return the chicken to skillet; heat through.

Spoon the chicken mixture onto warm tortillas; roll up. Top with favorite condiments. If desired, serve on a bed of shredded lettuce. Makes 4 servings.

Nutrition information per serving: 425 calories, 23 g protein, 45 g carbohydrate, 17 g fat (4 g saturated fat), 51 mg cholesterol, 600 mg sodium.

Polynesian Chicken Kabobs

Fresh pineapple adds a special flavor to these colorful kabobs. To save time and effort, look for peeled, fresh pineapple in the produce department of your supermarket.

1 pound skinless, boneless chicken breast halves or thighs
¼ cup soy sauce
2 tablespoons lemon juice
2 cloves garlic, minced
1 teaspoon grated gingerroot or ⅛ teaspoon ground ginger
⅛ teaspoon dry mustard
1 medium green sweet pepper
1 medium red sweet pepper
1 cup fresh pineapple chunks or one 8-ounce can pineapple chunks, drained
   Hot cooked rice (optional)
   Green onion fans (optional)

Rinse chicken; pat dry with paper towels. Cut into 1-inch pieces. Place chicken in a plastic bag and set the bag into a shallow dish. For marinade, in a small bowl combine soy sauce, lemon juice, garlic, ginger, and mustard. Pour over chicken; seal bag. Marinate in the refrigerator for 2 to 24 hours, turning bag occasionally.

Drain chicken, reserving marinade. Cut green and red peppers into 1-inch pieces. On 12 short metal skewers, alternately thread chicken, pineapple, green pepper, and red pepper.

Grill kabobs on an uncovered grill directly over medium coals for 12 to 14 minutes or until chicken is tender and no longer pink, turning and brushing once with marinade halfway through grilling.

(Or, in a covered grill arrange medium-hot coals around a drip pan. Test for medium heat above the pan. Place kabobs on grill rack over drip pan. Cover and grill for 16 to 18 minutes. Brush occasionally with marinade up to the last 5 minutes of grilling.)

If desired, serve the kabobs over hot cooked rice and garnish with green onion fans. Makes 6 servings.

Nutrition information per serving: 110 calories, 15 g protein, 7 g carbohydrate, 2 g fat (1 g saturated), 40 mg cholesterol, 723 mg sodium.

Pasta with Chicken and Pepper-Cheese Sauce

Ground red, white, and black and jalapeño peppers multiply the hotness by four in this zippy cream sauce.

8 ounces packaged dried spaghetti or fettuccine

3 small skinless, boneless chicken breast halves (about 8 ounces total)

1 tablespoon all-purpose flour

½ teaspoon salt

¼ to ½ teaspoon ground red pepper

⅛ to ¼ teaspoon ground white pepper

⅛ to ¼ teaspoon ground black pepper

1 tablespoon cooking oil

1 medium red or green sweet pepper, chopped (1 cup)

1 medium onion, chopped (½ cup)

1 tablespoon chopped, seeded jalapeño pepper

2 cloves garlic, minced

2 tablespoons all-purpose flour

¾ cup chicken broth

½ cup milk

1 teaspoon Worcestershire sauce

1 cup shredded Monterey Jack or cheddar cheese (4 ounces)

¼ cup dairy sour cream

1 jalapeño pepper, thinly sliced (optional)

Cook pasta according to package directions. Drain; keep warm.

Rinse chicken; pat dry with paper towels. Cut into 1-inch pieces. In a small mixing bowl combine the 1 tablespoon flour, salt, ground red pepper, white pepper, and black pepper. Toss flour mixture with chicken to coat. Set aside.

In a large skillet heat the oil over medium-high heat. (Add more oil as necessary during cooking.) Add sweet pepper, onion, chopped jalapeño pepper, and garlic; cook and stir until vegetables are tender. Remove the vegetables with a slotted spoon; set aside.

Add chicken to the skillet. Cook and stir for 3 to 4 minutes or until chicken is tender and no longer pink. Remove chicken from skillet.

Stir 2 tablespoons flour into drippings in skillet. Add chicken broth, milk, and Worcestershire sauce. Cook and stir until thickened and bubbly. Add the Monterey Jack or cheddar cheese, stirring until cheese melts. Stir 1 cup of the hot mixture into the sour cream; return all of the sour cream mixture to skillet. Stir in chicken and vegetables. Cook until heated through. Do not boil.

Arrange pasta on individual plates or a large platter. Spoon the chicken mixture over pasta. If desired, garnish with jalapeño pepper slices. Makes 4 servings.

Nutrition information per serving: 512 calories, 29 g protein, 56 g carbohydrate, 19 g fat (9 g saturated), 64 mg cholesterol, 660 mg sodium.

Chicken Manicotti with Chive-Cream Sauce

Broccoli and roasted red peppers or pimiento add vivid colors to the tasty chicken filling that spills from these pasta shells.

12 packaged dried manicotti shells
 1 8-ounce container soft-style cream
    cheese with chives and onion
⅔ cup milk
¼ cup grated Romano or Parmesan
    cheese
 2 cups chopped cooked chicken
    (10 ounces)
 1 10-ounce package frozen chopped
    broccoli, thawed and drained
½ of a 7-ounce jar roasted red
    sweet peppers, drained and sliced,
    or one 4-ounce jar diced
    pimiento, drained
¼ teaspoon black pepper
    Paprika

Cook manicotti shells according to package directions. Drain shells; rinse with cold water. Drain again.

Meanwhile, for sauce, in a small heavy saucepan melt cream cheese over medium-low heat, stirring constantly. Slowly add milk, stirring until smooth. Stir in Romano or Parmesan cheese. Remove from heat.

For filling, in a medium mixing bowl stir together ¾ cup of the sauce, chicken, broccoli, roasted red sweet peppers or pimiento, and black pepper. Using a small spoon, carefully fill each manicotti shell with about ⅓ cup of the filling.

Arrange the filled shells in a 3-quart rectangular baking dish. Pour the remaining sauce over the shells. Sprinkle with paprika. Cover with foil. Bake in a 350° oven for 25 to 30 minutes or until heated through. Makes 6 servings.

Nutrition information per serving: 396 calories, 25 g protein, 31 g carbohydrate, 18 g fat (9 g saturated), 92 mg cholesterol, 257 mg sodium.

QUICK-COOKED CHICKEN

If you need cooked chicken for a recipe but don't have any leftovers, one solution is to purchase a deli-roasted chicken. Or, poach chicken breasts. For 2 cups chopped cooked chicken, in a large skillet combine 12 ounces skinless, boneless chicken breast halves and 1½ cups water. Cover and simmer for 12 to 14 minutes or until tender and no longer pink. Drain and cut up chicken.

Deep-Dish Chicken Pie

To save time with the same delicious results, you can easily substitute one folded refrigerated unbaked piecrust for the Pastry for Single-Crust Pie. Just put the chicken mixture in a 2-quart round casserole and top with the piecrust. Flute, brush, and bake as directed in the recipe.

Pastry for Single-Crust Pie
- 3 medium leeks or 1 large onion, chopped
- 1 cup sliced fresh mushrooms
- ¾ cup sliced celery
- ½ cup chopped red sweet pepper
- 2 tablespoons margarine or butter
- ⅓ cup all-purpose flour
- 1 teaspoon poultry seasoning
- ¼ teaspoon salt
- ¼ teaspoon black pepper
- 1½ cups chicken broth
- 1 cup half-and-half, light cream, or milk
- 2½ cups chopped cooked chicken
- 1 cup frozen peas
- 1 slightly beaten egg

Prepare Pastry for Single-Crust Pie. On a lightly floured surface, roll pastry into a rectangle ⅛ inch thick. Trim to a rectangle 1 inch larger than a 2-quart rectangular baking dish. Using a sharp knife or small cookie cutter, cut some shapes out of center of pastry.

In a large saucepan cook leeks or onion, mushrooms, celery, and sweet pepper in margarine or butter over medium heat until tender. Stir in the flour, poultry seasoning, salt, and black pepper. Add the broth and half-and-half, light cream, or milk all at once. Cook and stir until thickened and bubbly. Stir in the cooked chicken and peas. Pour into the baking dish.

Place pastry over the hot chicken mixture in dish; turn edges of pastry under and flute to top edges of dish. Brush with the egg. Place reserved pastry shapes on top of pastry. Brush again with egg.

Bake in a 400° oven for 30 to 35 minutes or until the crust is golden brown. Cool about 20 minutes before serving. Makes 6 servings.

Pastry for Single-Crust Pie: In a medium bowl stir together 1¼ cups *all-purpose flour* and ¼ teaspoon *salt*. Using a pastry blender, cut in ⅓ cup *shortening* until pieces are pea-size. Using 4 to 5 tablespoons *cold water*, sprinkle 1 tablespoon water at a time over mixture, gently tossing with a fork until all is moistened. Form dough into a ball.

Nutrition information per serving: 484 calories, 27 g protein, 35 g carbohydrate, 26 g fat (8 g saturated fat), 107 mg cholesterol, 538 mg sodium.

Turkey Breast with Raspberry Salsa

Raspberry jam and prepared salsa team up for a sweet sauce with just a little kick.

⅓ cup seedless raspberry jam
1 tablespoon Dijon-style mustard
1 teaspoon finely shredded orange peel
½ cup mild salsa
1 2- to 2½-pound bone-in turkey breast half
  Orange peel strips (optional)

Stir together raspberry jam, mustard, and 1 teaspoon orange peel. Stir 3 tablespoons of the jam mixture into salsa. Cover and chill jam mixture and salsa mixture. If desired, skin turkey breast. Rinse turkey; pat dry with paper towels. Insert a meat thermometer into the center of turkey breast.

In a covered grill arrange medium-hot coals around a drip pan. Test for medium heat above the pan. Place turkey, bone side down, on grill rack over drip pan. Cover and grill for 1 to 1¼ hours or until meat thermometer registers 170°, brushing occasionally with jam mixture during the last 30 minutes of grilling.

Remove turkey from grill and cover with foil. Let stand for 15 minutes before slicing. Serve turkey with salsa mixture. If desired, garnish with orange peel strips. Makes 8 servings.

Nutrition information per serving: 149 calories, 20 g protein, 11 g carbohydrate, 3 g fat (1 g saturated), 46 mg cholesterol, 147 mg sodium.

*H*ANDLING POULTRY SAFELY

Follow these simple guidelines to safely handle fresh poultry.
• Always wash your hands, work surfaces, and utensils in hot soapy water after handling raw poultry to prevent spreading bacteria to other foods.
• When cutting raw poultry, use a plastic cutting board because it's easier to clean and disinfect than a wooden one.
• When grilling, never use the same plate to transfer raw and cooked poultry to and from the grill.
• Always marinate poultry in the refrigerator.
• Serve poultry immediately after cooking it. Refrigerate leftovers as soon as possible.

Stuffed Turkey Tenderloins

There's more than one way to stuff a turkey. Fresh spinach and tangy goat cheese make a melt-in-your-mouth filling in these turkey tenderloins. When sliced, the rosy-red, spicy crust on the meat yields to a juicy, tender interior.

2   8-ounce turkey breast tenderloins
2   cups chopped spinach leaves
3   ounces semisoft goat cheese
      (chèvre) or feta cheese, crumbled
      (about ¾ cup)
½   teaspoon black pepper
1   tablespoon olive oil
1   teaspoon paprika
½   teaspoon salt
⅛   to ¼ teaspoon ground red pepper

Rinse turkey; pat dry with paper towels. Make a pocket in each tenderloin by cutting lengthwise from one side almost to, but not through, the opposite side. Set aside.

For stuffing, in a medium bowl combine spinach, goat or feta cheese, and black pepper. Spoon stuffing into pockets. Tie 100% cotton string around each tenderloin in 3 or 4 places to hold in stuffing. In a small bowl combine oil, paprika, salt, and ground red pepper. Brush evenly over turkey.

Grill turkey on lightly greased rack of an uncovered grill directly over medium coals for 16 to 20 minutes or until turkey is tender and no longer pink in center of the thickest part, turning once.

Remove and discard the strings. Slice turkey tenderloins crosswise. Makes 4 servings.

Nutrition information per serving: 220 calories, 26 g protein, 1 g carbohydrate, 12 g fat (4 g saturated), 68 mg cholesterol, 458 mg sodium.

*C*LEANING YOUR GRILL

To make the job easier, clean your grill rack right after cooking. Let it cool until easily handled, then soak it in hot sudsy water to loosen cooked-on grime. If the rack is too large for your sink, let it stand about 1 hour wrapped in wet paper towels, then wipe clean. If necessary, use a stiff brush to remove stubborn burned-on food.

Pineapple-Orange Ginger Turkey

This easy-to-fix Polynesian-style dish capitalizes on the tangy-sweet flavors of pineapple and orange juice concentrate plus a generous amount of fresh ginger.

1 pound turkey breast tenderloin
  steaks
2 tablespoons soy sauce
2 tablespoons dry sherry
½ of a 6-ounce can (⅓ cup) frozen
  orange juice concentrate, thawed
2 tablespoons soy sauce
1 tablespoon water
2 teaspoons cornstarch
½ teaspoon sugar
1 tablespoon cooking oil
2 to 3 teaspoons grated gingerroot
1 medium red or green sweet pepper,
  cut into bite-size strips
1 8-ounce can pineapple chunks
  (juice pack), drained
2 cups hot cooked rice
  Orange slices (optional)
  Fresh rosemary sprigs (optional)

Rinse turkey; pat dry with paper towels. Cut into thin bite-size strips. In a medium bowl stir together turkey, 2 tablespoons soy sauce, and sherry. Cover and chill for 30 minutes to 1 hour.

For sauce, in a small bowl stir together the orange juice concentrate, 2 tablespoons soy sauce, water, cornstarch, and sugar. Set aside.

Add cooking oil to a wok or large skillet. Preheat over medium-high heat (add more oil if necessary during cooking). Stir-fry gingerroot in hot oil for 15 seconds. Add pepper strips; stir-fry for 1 to 2 minutes or until crisp-tender. Remove pepper strips from wok.

Add half of the turkey mixture to wok. Stir-fry for 2 to 3 minutes or until turkey is tender and no longer pink. Remove turkey from wok. Repeat with the remaining turkey mixture. Return all of the turkey to wok. Push turkey from center of wok.

Stir sauce; add to center of wok. Cook and stir until thickened and bubbly. Return pepper strips to wok. Add pineapple. Stir all ingredients together to coat. Cook and stir about 1 minute more or until mixture is heated through.

Serve immediately with hot rice. If desired, garnish with orange slices and rosemary. Makes 4 servings.

Nutrition information per serving: 352 calories, 25 g protein, 46 g carbohydrate, 6 g fat (1 g saturated fat), 50 mg cholesterol, 1,077 mg sodium.

Turkey Lasagna Rolls

For this robust lasagna-style entrée, roll the noodles around a cheesy spinach filling and then top them with a ground turkey and tomato sauce.

8	ounces ground raw turkey
1	medium onion, chopped (½ cup)
2	cloves garlic, minced
1	cup sliced fresh mushrooms
1	cup water
1	7½-ounce can tomatoes, cut up
1	6-ounce can tomato paste
1½	teaspoons dried oregano, crushed
1	teaspoon dried basil, crushed
8	packaged dried lasagna noodles
1	beaten egg
1	15-ounce carton ricotta cheese
1	10-ounce package frozen chopped spinach, thawed and drained
1½	cups shredded mozzarella cheese (6 ounces)
1	cup grated Parmesan cheese
	Fresh parsley sprigs (optional)

For sauce, in a large skillet cook turkey, onion, and garlic until turkey is no longer pink; drain fat. Stir in mushrooms, water, undrained tomatoes, tomato paste, oregano, and basil. Bring to boiling; reduce heat. Cover and simmer for 25 minutes.

Meanwhile, cook the lasagna noodles according to package directions. Drain noodles; rinse with cold water. Drain again.

For filling, in a mixing bowl stir together egg, ricotta cheese, spinach, 1 cup of the mozzarella cheese, and ¾ cup of the Parmesan cheese.

To assemble rolls, spread about ½ cup of the filling over each lasagna noodle. Roll up noodles, starting from a short end. Place lasagna rolls, seam sides down, in a 2-quart rectangular baking dish. Pour sauce over lasagna rolls. Cover dish with foil.

Bake in a 375° oven for 25 minutes. Remove foil. Sprinkle with remaining mozzarella cheese. Bake for 5 to 10 minutes more or until heated through. Let stand 5 minutes before serving. Sprinkle with remaining Parmesan cheese and, if desired, garnish with parsley sprigs. Makes 8 servings.

Nutrition information per serving: 345 calories, 26 g protein, 28 g carbohydrate, 15 g fat (8 g saturated), 75 mg cholesterol, 511 mg sodium.

Herbed Turkey and Broccoli

Soft-style cream cheese makes an ultra-rich sauce for this one-pan pasta dish.

8   ounces packaged dried linguine or
      spaghetti, broken in half
3   cups small broccoli flowerets
1   8-ounce container soft-style cream
      cheese with garlic and herbs
⅔   cup milk
¼   teaspoon coarsely ground pepper
6   ounces sliced fully cooked smoked
      turkey breast, cut into bite-size
      strips

In a 4½-quart Dutch oven cook pasta in boiling water for 6 minutes. Add broccoli. Return to boiling. Cook for 2 to 3 minutes more or until pasta is tender and broccoli is crisp-tender. Drain in a colander.

In the same Dutch oven combine cream cheese, milk, and pepper. Cook and stir over low heat until cream cheese is melted. Add pasta mixture and turkey. Toss to coat. If necessary, stir in additional milk to make desired consistency. Makes 4 servings.

Nutrition information per serving: 516 calories, 25 g protein, 57 g carbohydrate, 21 g fat (11 g saturated), 81 mg cholesterol, 675 mg sodium.

Grilled Turkey Burgers

Who says beef has to make the all-American burger? We gave the classic burger a makeover by using ground turkey, glazing it with orange marmalade, and serving it on rye or wheat buns.

1   beaten egg
⅓   cup fine dry bread crumbs
¼   cup finely chopped green sweet
      pepper
2   green onions, finely chopped
2   tablespoons milk
½   teaspoon salt
⅛   teaspoon black pepper
1   pound ground raw turkey
2   tablespoons orange marmalade
5   rye or wheat sandwich buns, split
      Shredded lettuce (optional)
      Tomato slices, halved (optional)
      Onion slices (optional)

In a medium mixing bowl combine egg, bread crumbs, green pepper, chopped green onions, milk, salt, and black pepper. Add ground turkey; mix well. Shape mixture into five ¾-inch-thick patties.

Grill patties on an uncovered grill directly over medium coals for 14 to 18 minutes or until done (165°), turning and brushing once with orange marmalade.

(Or, in a covered grill arrange medium-hot coals around a drip pan. Test for medium heat above the pan. Place patties on grill rack over drip pan. Cover and grill for 20 to 24 minutes, turning and brushing once with orange marmalade.)

Toast cut sides of buns on grill. Serve patties in buns and, if desired, with lettuce, tomato, and onion slices. Makes 5 servings.

Nutrition information per serving: 289 calories, 17 g protein, 30 g carbohydrate, 11 g fat (2 g saturated), 77 mg cholesterol, 396 mg sodium.

Spaghetti with Turkey Meatballs

We updated everyone's favorite pasta dish by using ground turkey instead of ground beef.

1 large onion, chopped (1 cup)
1 medium green sweet pepper, coarsely chopped (1 cup)
1 medium carrot, coarsely chopped (½ cup)
1 stalk celery, sliced (½ cup)
1 tablespoon cooking oil
4 large ripe tomatoes, peeled and chopped (4 cups), or two 14½-ounce cans tomatoes, cut up
1 6-ounce can (⅔ cup) tomato paste
2 teaspoons dried Italian seasoning, crushed
½ teaspoon sugar
½ teaspoon salt
½ teaspoon garlic powder
   Turkey Meatballs
12 ounces packaged dried spaghetti or mostaccioli

For sauce, in a Dutch oven cook onion, green pepper, carrot, and celery in hot oil until tender. Stir in fresh or undrained canned tomatoes, tomato paste, Italian seasoning, sugar, salt, and garlic powder. Bring to boiling.

Add the Turkey Meatballs; reduce heat. Cover and simmer for 30 minutes. If necessary, uncover and simmer for 10 to 15 minutes more or until sauce is desired consistency, stirring occasionally.

Meanwhile, cook the pasta according to package directions. Drain.

Arrange pasta on individual plates or a large platter. Spoon the meatballs and sauce over pasta. Makes 6 servings.

Turkey Meatballs: In a medium mixing bowl combine 1 beaten *egg* and 2 tablespoons *milk*. Stir in ¼ cup *fine dry bread crumbs;* ½ teaspoon *salt;* ½ teaspoon *dried Italian seasoning,* crushed; and ½ teaspoon *pepper*. Add 1 pound *ground raw turkey;* mix well. With wet hands, shape mixture into twenty-four 1-inch meatballs. Place the meatballs in a greased 13x9x2-inch baking pan. Bake in a 375° oven about 20 minutes or until turkey is done (165°). Drain fat.

Nutrition information per serving: 442 calories, 22 g protein, 65 g carbohydrate, 11 g fat (2 g saturated), 64 mg cholesterol, 686 mg sodium.

Fish
& SEAFOOD

Contents

PAN-SEARED SCALLOPS
(recipe, page 181)

Grilled Tuna with Tuscan Beans

Tuna and beans—tonno e fagioli—is a favorite combination in Italian coastal towns. Using canned beans makes our version fast and easy.

1 pound fresh or frozen tuna,
    swordfish, halibut, shark, or
    salmon steaks
2 cloves garlic, minced
1 tablespoon olive oil
1 14½-ounce can Italian-style stewed
    tomatoes, cut up
2 teaspoons snipped fresh sage or
    ¼ teaspoon ground sage
1 15-ounce can small white beans,
    rinsed and drained
2 teaspoons olive oil
2 teaspoons lemon juice
⅛ teaspoon pepper
    Fresh sage sprigs (optional)

Thaw fish, if frozen. In a large skillet cook the garlic in 1 tablespoon hot oil for 15 seconds. Stir in the undrained tomatoes and snipped fresh or dried sage. Bring to boiling; reduce heat. Simmer, uncovered, for 5 minutes. Stir in beans; heat through.

Meanwhile, rinse fish; pat dry with paper towels. Cut fish into 4 serving-size portions. Brush both sides of fish with the 2 teaspoons oil and the lemon juice. Sprinkle with pepper.

Grill fish on the greased rack of an uncovered grill directly over medium coals until fish flakes easily with a fork, gently turning once (allow 4 to 6 minutes per ½-inch thickness).

[Or, place fish on the greased unheated rack of a broiler pan. Broil 4 inches from heat, gently turning once (allow 4 to 6 minutes per ½-inch thickness).]

To serve, remove the skin from fish. Spoon the bean mixture onto dinner plates and top with fish. If desired, garnish with sage sprigs. Makes 4 servings.

Nutrition information per serving: 298 calories, 33 g protein, 25 g carbohydrate, 7 g fat (1 g saturated), 49 mg cholesterol, 536 mg sodium.

Poached Orange Roughy with Lemon Sauce

Despite its speed, poaching is an inherently gentle way to cook. It's also one of the lightest and most healthful. Here, poaching in lemon- and pepper-infused broth preserves the delicate flavor and texture of one of the most popular kinds of white fish.

1 pound fresh or frozen orange roughy or red snapper fillets, about ½ inch thick
1 pound asparagus
1 14½-ounce can reduced-sodium chicken broth
2 teaspoons finely shredded lemon peel
⅛ teaspoon black pepper
1 medium yellow sweet pepper, cut into bite-size strips
4 teaspoons cornstarch
2 tablespoons snipped fresh chives
2 cups hot cooked couscous or rice

Thaw fish, if frozen. Rinse fish. Cut the fish into 4 serving-size portions; set aside. Snap off and discard woody bases from asparagus. Cut asparagus in half.

In a large skillet combine 1 cup of the broth, the lemon peel, and black pepper. Bring to boiling; reduce heat. Carefully add the fish and asparagus. Cover and cook over medium-low heat for 4 minutes. Add yellow pepper. Cover and cook about 2 minutes more or until fish flakes easily with a fork. Using a slotted spatula, remove fish and vegetables; reserve liquid in skillet. Keep fish and vegetables warm.

For sauce, stir together the remaining broth and cornstarch. Stir into liquid in skillet. Cook and stir until thickened and bubbly. Cook and stir for 2 minutes more. Stir in chives. Arrange fish and vegetables on hot couscous or rice; top with sauce. Makes 4 servings.

Nutrition information per serving: 249 calories, 28 g protein, 29 g carbohydrate, 2 g fat (0 g saturated), 60 mg cholesterol, 390 mg sodium.

𝒯HAWING FISH

To thaw fish, place the unopened package in a container in the refrigerator and allow overnight thawing for a 1-pound package. If necessary, you can place the wrapped package of fish under cold running water for 1 to 2 minutes to hasten thawing. Thawing fish at room temperature or in warm water isn't recommended, since the fish won't thaw evenly and may spoil. Do not refreeze fish.

Pesto Sole Roll-Ups

Walleyed pike is often called the "sole" of fresh waters and has long been a favorite of fishermen. It works equally as well as sole or flounder in these carrot and pesto filled bundles.

4 4-ounce fresh or frozen sole or
    flounder fillets, ¼ to ½ inch thick
⅔ cup refrigerated pesto sauce
1 medium carrot, shredded (½ cup)
1 tablespoon margarine or butter,
    melted
3 tablespoons fine dry bread crumbs
1 teaspoon finely shredded lemon peel
6 ounces hot cooked fettuccine
1 tablespoon lemon juice
    Lemon wedges (optional)
    Carrot curls (optional)
    Fresh basil sprigs (optional)

Thaw fish, if frozen. Rinse fish; pat dry with paper towels. Spread one side of each fillet with about 1 tablespoon of the pesto. Sprinkle each fillet with 2 tablespoons of the shredded carrot. Starting from a short end, roll up fish around the carrot. Place fish rolls, seam sides down, in a 2-quart square baking dish. Brush fish rolls with melted margarine or butter.

Toss together bread crumbs and lemon peel; sprinkle over fish rolls. Bake, uncovered, in a 375° oven for 20 to 25 minutes or until fish flakes easily with a fork.

Toss together the remaining pesto, hot pasta, and lemon juice. Divide the pasta mixture evenly among dinner plates and top each with a fish roll. If desired, garnish with lemon wedges, carrot curls, and basil sprigs. Makes 4 servings.

Nutrition information per serving: 607 calories, 31 g protein, 47 g carbohydrate, 32 g fat (1 g saturated), 59 mg cholesterol, 475 mg sodium.

SOONER IS BETTER

For best results, purchase fresh fish the same day you plan to cook it. When that's not possible, wrap the fish loosely in clear plastic wrap, store it in the coldest part of the refrigerator, and use it within 2 days. If you purchase frozen fish, keep it in a freezer set at 0° or lower for up to 3 months.

Halibut with Creamy Dijon Sauce

Feel like having a barbecue instead of cooking these fish steaks indoors? Grill the fish on a greased rack of an uncovered grill directly over medium coals for 8 to 12 minutes or until fish is done, turning fish and brushing once with the basting sauce.

4   fresh or frozen halibut or sea bass steaks, cut 1 inch thick (about 1½ pounds)
1   tablespoon margarine or butter, melted
¼   teaspoon onion salt
¼   teaspoon dried marjoram, crushed
¼   teaspoon dried thyme, crushed
½   cup dairy sour cream
1   tablespoon all-purpose flour
1   tablespoon Dijon-style mustard
⅛   teaspoon salt
⅛   teaspoon pepper
⅛   teaspoon dried thyme, crushed
½   cup chicken or vegetable broth
4   cups shredded spinach (5 ounces)
1   medium carrot, shredded (½ cup)
    Lemon wedges (optional)

Thaw fish, if frozen. Rinse fish; pat dry with paper towels. Set aside.

For basting sauce, combine margarine or butter, onion salt, marjoram, and ¼ teaspoon thyme.

Place fish steaks on the rack of an unheated broiler pan. Brush with basting sauce. Broil 4 inches from the heat for 8 to 12 minutes or until fish flakes easily with a fork, turning and brushing once with the remaining basting sauce halfway through broiling.

Meanwhile, for Dijon sauce, in a small saucepan stir together the sour cream, flour, mustard, salt, pepper, and ⅛ teaspoon thyme. Add chicken or vegetable broth, stirring until well mixed. Cook and stir over medium heat till thickened and bubbly. Cook and stir for 1 minute more. Keep warm.

Toss together spinach and carrot. Line dinner plates with the spinach mixture. Arrange fish on spinach mixture. Top with Dijon sauce. If desired, garnish with lemon wedges. Makes 4 servings.

Nutrition information per serving: 282 calories, 39 g protein, 9 g carbohydrate, 9 g fat (2 g saturated), 59 mg cholesterol, 549 mg sodium.

Salmon with Wilted Greens

This dinner packs in all the vitamin C and almost half of the vitamin A you need for an entire day—all for under 300 calories.

4   fresh or frozen salmon steaks, cut
       ¾ inch thick (about 1 pound)
3   tablespoons orange juice concentrate
3   tablespoons water
2   tablespoons reduced-sodium
       soy sauce
1   tablespoon honey
2   teaspoons cooking oil
1   teaspoon toasted sesame oil
½   teaspoon grated gingerroot or
       ¼ teaspoon ground ginger
6   cups torn mixed greens (such as
       spinach, Swiss chard, radicchio, or
       mustard, beet, or collard greens)
1   small red sweet pepper, cut into
       thin strips
1   medium orange, peeled and
       sectioned
    Orange peel strips (optional)

Thaw fish, if frozen. For dressing, in a small bowl combine orange juice concentrate, water, soy sauce, honey, cooking oil, toasted sesame oil, and ginger.

Rinse fish; pat dry with paper towels. Place the fish on the greased unheated rack of a broiler pan. Broil 4 inches from the heat for 3 minutes. Using a wide spatula, carefully turn fish. Brush with 1 tablespoon of the dressing. Broil for 3 to 6 minutes more or until fish flakes easily with a fork.

(Or, grill fish on the greased rack of an uncovered grill directly over medium coals for 3 minutes. Carefully turn fish. Brush with 1 tablespoon of the dressing. Grill for 3 to 6 minutes more.)

Remove fish. Cover and keep warm. Place the greens in a large salad bowl. In a large skillet bring the remaining dressing to boiling. Add red pepper strips. Remove from heat. Pour over greens, tossing to coat.

To serve, divide greens mixture among dinner plates. Arrange the orange sections and fish on top of greens. If desired, garnish with orange peel strips. Serve immediately. Makes 4 servings.

Nutrition information per serving: 255 calories, 27 g protein, 15 g carbohydrate, 9 g fat (2 g saturated), 31 mg cholesterol, 406 mg sodium.

Shark and Shrimp with Broccoli

Shark, marlin, and swordfish are excellent choices for stir-frying because of their firm texture.

8 ounces fresh or frozen shark, marlin, or swordfish steaks, cut 1 inch thick
8 ounces fresh or frozen, peeled, deveined medium shrimp
2 tablespoons soy sauce
2 tablespoons dry sherry
1 teaspoon grated gingerroot
¾ teaspoon sugar
1 tablespoon cooking oil
1 clove garlic, minced
4 cups broccoli flowerets
1 medium red or green sweet pepper, chopped
2 cups hot cooked Chinese egg noodles or fine noodles

Thaw fish and shrimp, if frozen. Rinse fish and shrimp; pat dry with paper towels. Cut fish into 1-inch cubes. Discard any skin and bones.

In a medium bowl stir together fish, shrimp, soy sauce, sherry, gingerroot, and sugar. Cover and marinate in the refrigerator for 30 minutes. Drain fish and shrimp, reserving marinade. Set aside.

Add cooking oil to a wok or large skillet. Preheat over medium-high heat (add more oil if necessary during cooking). Stir-fry garlic in hot oil for 15 seconds. Add broccoli; stir-fry for 3 minutes. Add sweet pepper; stir-fry about 1 minute more or until vegetables are crisp-tender. Remove vegetables from wok.

Add half of the fish and shrimp to wok. Stir-fry for 3 to 5 minutes or until fish flakes easily with a fork, being careful not to break up pieces. Remove from wok. Repeat with the remaining fish and shrimp. Return all of the fish and shrimp to wok. Push fish and shrimp from center of wok.

Add marinade to center of wok. Cook and stir until bubbly. Return cooked vegetables to wok. Gently stir all ingredients together to coat. Cook and stir for 1 to 2 minutes more or until heated through. Serve immediately over hot noodles. Makes 4 servings.

Nutrition information per serving: 298 calories, 28 g protein, 28 g carbohydrate, 8 g fat (2 g saturated fat), 136 mg cholesterol, 695 mg sodium.

Fish Creole

For a refreshingly light entrée, stir-fry fish with the classic flavors of New Orleans—green pepper, celery, onion, and tomatoes.

1   pound fresh or frozen swordfish,
      sea bass, tuna, or tilefish steaks,
      cut 1 inch thick
1   14½-ounce can tomatoes, cut up
½   teaspoon sugar
½   teaspoon salt
⅛   to ¼ teaspoon ground red pepper
1   tablespoon cooking oil
1   medium onion, chopped
1   stalk celery, thinly sliced
1   medium green sweet pepper, cut
      into 2-inch strips
2   tablespoons snipped parsley
2   cups hot cooked rice

Thaw fish, if frozen. Rinse fish; pat dry with paper towels. Cut into 1-inch cubes. Discard any skin and bones. Set aside.

In a small bowl stir together undrained tomatoes, sugar, salt, and ground red pepper. Set aside.

Add cooking oil to a wok or large skillet. Preheat over medium-high heat (add more oil if necessary during cooking). Stir-fry onion and celery in hot oil for 2 minutes. Add sweet pepper strips; stir-fry about 2 minutes more or until vegetables are crisp-tender. Remove the vegetables from wok.

Add half of the fish cubes to wok. Stir-fry for 3 to 5 minutes or until fish flakes easily with a fork, being careful not to break up pieces. Remove from wok. Repeat with the remaining fish cubes. Remove all of the fish from wok.

Add the tomato mixture to wok. Return the cooked vegetables to wok. Stir all ingredients together to coat. Cook and stir about 3 minutes or until slightly thickened. Add parsley. Gently stir in fish. Cook for 1 to 2 minutes more or until heated through. Serve immediately in bowls over hot rice. Makes 4 servings.

Nutrition information per serving: 311 calories, 26 g protein, 31 g carbohydrate, 9 g fat (2 g saturated fat), 45 mg cholesterol, 569 mg sodium.

Nutty Parmesan Fish

A light and crispy coating that features cracker crumbs, pine nuts, and Parmesan cheese makes a flavor-packed breading for these oven-fried fish sticks.

1	**pound fresh or frozen orange roughy or haddock fillets**
1	**beaten egg**
2	**tablespoons milk**
¼	**cup finely crushed rich round crackers**
2	**tablespoons grated Parmesan cheese**
2	**tablespoons ground pine nuts or almonds**
½	**teaspoon dried basil, crushed**
⅛	**teaspoon pepper**
2	**tablespoons margarine or butter, melted**
	Tartar Sauce (optional)

Thaw fish, if frozen. Rinse fish; pat dry with paper towels. Cut fish into 1-inch-wide strips. Set aside.

In a shallow dish combine egg and milk. In another shallow dish combine cracker crumbs, Parmesan cheese, ground nuts, basil, and pepper. Dip fish pieces into egg mixture and then roll in crumb mixture. Place coated fish in a greased shallow baking pan. Drizzle melted margarine or butter over fish.

Bake in a 500° oven until coating is golden and fish flakes easily with a fork (allow 4 to 6 minutes per ½-inch thickness). If desired, serve with Tartar Sauce. Makes 4 servings.

Tartar Sauce: In a small bowl stir together 1 cup *mayonnaise* or *salad dressing,* ¼ cup finely chopped *dill pickle* or *sweet pickle relish,* 1 tablespoon sliced *green onion,* 1 tablespoon snipped *parsley,* 1 tablespoon diced *pimiento,* and 1 teaspoon *lemon juice.* Cover and chill until serving time. Makes about 1 cup.

Nutrition information per serving: 221 calories, 22 g protein, 5 g carbohydrate, 13 g fat (3 g saturated), 80 mg cholesterol, 267 mg sodium.

Shopping for Fish Fillets

Trust your eyes and nose when buying fish fillets. Look for firm, moist, clean-cut fillets. Avoid those that have a strong or fishy odor and ragged edges.

Deep-Dish Tuna Pie

A convenient, off-the-shelf piecrust mix makes a flaky top that looks and tastes like you made it from scratch.

½ of an 11-ounce package piecrust mix (1⅓ cups)
1 large onion, chopped (1 cup)
1 medium potato, peeled and chopped (about 1 cup)
1 10¾-ounce can condensed cream of mushroom soup
⅓ cup grated Parmesan cheese
⅓ cup milk
1 tablespoon lemon juice
¾ teaspoon dried dillweed
¼ teaspoon pepper
1 16-ounce package frozen mixed vegetables
1 9¼-ounce can tuna, drained and broken into chunks
1 beaten egg

Prepare piecrust mix according to package directions, except do not roll out. Cover dough; set aside.

In a covered large skillet cook onion and potato in a small amount of boiling water about 7 minutes or until tender. Drain. Stir in soup, Parmesan cheese, milk, lemon juice, dillweed, and pepper. Cook and stir until mixture is bubbly. Gently stir in the frozen mixed vegetables and tuna. Spoon mixture into an ungreased 2-quart round casserole.

On a lightly floured surface, roll pastry into a circle 2 inches larger than the diameter of the top of the casserole and about ⅛ inch thick. Make 1-inch slits near the center of the pastry. Center pastry over top of casserole, allowing ends to hang over edge. Trim pastry ½ inch beyond edge of casserole. Turn pastry under; flute to the casserole edge, pressing gently. Brush pastry with beaten egg.

Bake in a 400° oven for 40 to 45 minutes or until crust is golden brown. Serve immediately. Makes 6 servings.

Nutrition information per serving: 386 calories, 21 g protein, 35 g carbohydrate, 18 g fat (5 g saturated), 49 mg cholesterol, 893 mg sodium.

CHOPPED ONIONS THE EASY WAY

To chop onions quickly, first cut the onion in half. Use the cut side as a base to stabilize the piece. Slice the onion half in one direction; holding the slices together with one hand, slice in the other direction. The job is easier if you use a chef's knife because it's designed to let you grasp the handle without your fingers touching the cutting surface.

Seafood Enchiladas

Imitation seafood is made commercially by processing and re-forming minced fish to look like shellfish. It's less expensive than crab or lobster and, as an added bonus, is lower in cholesterol.

8   6-inch corn tortillas
1   medium red onion, finely chopped
      (½ cup)
2   cloves garlic, minced
1   teaspoon ground coriander
¼   teaspoon black pepper
2   tablespoons margarine or butter
3   tablespoons all-purpose flour
1   8-ounce carton dairy sour cream
1   14½-ounce can chicken broth
1   or 2 canned jalapeño peppers,
      rinsed, seeded, and chopped, or
      one 4-ounce can diced green chile
      peppers, drained
1   cup shredded Monterey Jack cheese
      (4 ounces)
12 ounces flake-style imitation
      crabmeat
    Chopped tomatoes (optional)
    Cilantro sprigs (optional)

Wrap corn tortillas in foil. Heat in a 350° oven for 10 to 15 minutes or until softened.

Meanwhile, for sauce, in a medium saucepan cook the onion, garlic, coriander, and black pepper in margarine or butter over medium heat until onion is tender. In a medium bowl stir flour into sour cream; stir in broth. Add the sour cream mixture to onion mixture. Stir in jalapeño or green chile peppers. Cook and stir until mixture is slightly thickened and bubbly. Remove from heat. Add half of the cheese, stirring until melted.

For filling, stir ½ cup of the sauce into crabmeat. Place about ¼ cup of the filling on each tortilla; roll up. Arrange tortilla rolls, seam sides down, in a lightly greased 2-quart rectangular baking dish. Top with the remaining sauce. Bake, covered, in a 350° oven for 30 to 35 minutes or until heated through.

Sprinkle with the remaining cheese. Bake, uncovered, about 5 minutes more or until cheese is melted. Let stand for 10 minutes before serving. If desired, garnish with tomatoes, cilantro, and additional finely chopped red onion. Makes 4 servings.

Nutrition information per serving: 550 calories, 26 g protein, 44 g carbohydrate, 30 g fat (15 g saturated), 68 mg cholesterol, 1,461 mg sodium.

Shrimp Curry

Tease your taste buds with this invigorating alliance of sweet raisins and hot pepper sauce.

12	ounces fresh or frozen, peeled, deveined shrimp
1	large onion, chopped (1 cup)
1	medium green sweet pepper, cut into 1-inch pieces (1 cup)
1	stalk celery, sliced (½ cup)
1	clove garlic, minced
2	tablespoons cooking oil
1	14½-ounce can tomatoes, cut up
½	cup slivered almonds
½	cup raisins
¼	cup snipped parsley
¼	cup chili sauce
1	teaspoon lemon juice
½	teaspoon salt
½	teaspoon bottled hot pepper sauce
¼	teaspoon white pepper
¼	teaspoon curry powder
¼	teaspoon dried thyme, crushed
2	cups hot cooked rice
¼	cup slivered almonds, toasted

Thaw shrimp, if frozen. Rinse the shrimp; pat dry with paper towels. Set aside.

In a 12-inch skillet cook onion, green pepper, celery, and garlic in hot oil until crisp-tender. Stir in undrained tomatoes, ½ cup almonds, raisins, parsley, chili sauce, lemon juice, salt, hot pepper sauce, white pepper, curry powder, and thyme. Bring to boiling; reduce heat. Cover and simmer for 30 minutes.

Stir shrimp into tomato mixture. Return to boiling; reduce heat. Cover and simmer about 5 minutes more or until shrimp turn pink. Serve over rice. Sprinkle each serving with toasted almonds. Makes 4 servings.

Nutrition information per serving: 511 calories, 24 g protein, 63 g carbohydrate, 20 g fat (2 g saturated), 131 mg cholesterol, 841 mg sodium.

*P*EELING AND DEVEINING SHRIMP

To peel and devein shrimp, first open the shell of each shrimp lengthwise down the body. Start at the head and peel away the shell. Gently pull on the tail to remove it. Using a sharp knife, make a shallow slit along the back from the head to the tail. Locate the black vein. If the vein is exposed, hold the shrimp under cold running water; rinse away the vein. If it isn't, remove vein using the tip of a knife, then rinse.

Spicy Shrimp on Skewers

For a tangy accompaniment to the peppery shrimp, add fresh pineapple wedges to the grill alongside the shrimp during the last 5 minutes of grilling.

1½	pounds fresh or frozen large shrimp in shells
½	cup frozen pineapple juice concentrate, thawed
1	to 2 tablespoons finely chopped jalapeño peppers
1	teaspoon grated gingerroot or ⅛ teaspoon ground ginger
1	clove garlic, minced
¼	teaspoon crushed red pepper Hot cooked rice pilaf (optional)

Thaw shrimp, if frozen. Peel and devein shrimp. Rinse shrimp; pat dry with paper towels. Place shrimp in a plastic bag and set the bag into a shallow dish.

For marinade, in a small mixing bowl combine the pineapple juice concentrate, jalapeño peppers, ginger, garlic, and crushed red pepper. Pour over shrimp; seal bag. Marinate in the refrigerator for 1 to 2 hours, turning bag once.

Drain the shrimp, reserving marinade. Thread shrimp onto 5 long metal skewers.

Grill kabobs on an uncovered grill directly over medium coals for 6 to 8 minutes or until shrimp turn pink, turning and brushing once with marinade halfway through grilling.

(Or, in a covered grill arrange medium-hot coals around a drip pan. Test for medium heat above the pan. Place kabobs on grill rack over drip pan. Cover and grill for 8 to 10 minutes, brushing occasionally with marinade during the first half of grilling.)

If desired, serve the shrimp kabobs over hot cooked rice pilaf. Makes 5 servings.

Nutrition information per serving: 133 calories, 17 g protein, 13 g carbohydrate, 1 g fat (0 g saturated), 157 mg cholesterol, 181 mg sodium.

Fettuccine with Herbed Shrimp

A white wine and herb sauce dresses the shrimp and pasta in this elegant entrée.

12	ounces fresh or frozen, peeled, deveined shrimp
6	ounces packaged dried plain and/or spinach fettuccine
2	cups sliced fresh mushrooms
1	large onion, chopped (1 cup)
2	cloves garlic, minced
1	tablespoon olive oil or cooking oil
¼	cup dry white wine
1	tablespoon instant chicken bouillon granules
1	tablespoon snipped fresh basil or 1 teaspoon dried basil, crushed
1½	teaspoons snipped fresh oregano or ½ teaspoon dried oregano, crushed
1	teaspoon cornstarch
⅛	teaspoon pepper
2	medium tomatoes, peeled, seeded, and chopped
¼	cup grated Parmesan cheese
¼	cup snipped parsley

Thaw shrimp, if frozen. Rinse shrimp; pat dry with paper towels. Cut shrimp in half lengthwise; set aside.

Cook pasta according to package directions. Drain; keep warm.

Meanwhile, in a large saucepan cook mushrooms, onion, and garlic in hot oil until onion is tender.

In a small mixing bowl stir together wine, bouillon granules, basil, oregano, cornstarch, and pepper. Add to mushroom mixture. Cook and stir until thickened and bubbly.

Add shrimp to mushroom mixture. Cover and simmer about 2 minutes or until shrimp turn pink. Stir in tomatoes; heat through.

Spoon the shrimp mixture over pasta. Sprinkle with Parmesan cheese and parsley. Toss to coat. Makes 4 servings.

Nutrition information per serving: 351 calories, 25 g protein, 44 g carbohydrate, 7 g fat (2 g saturated), 136 mg cholesterol, 926 mg sodium.

Selecting Shrimp

At fish markets or supermarket fish counters, shrimp is usually sold by the pound. The price per pound is determined by size—the bigger the shrimp, the higher the price and the fewer per pound. Select fresh shrimp that are moist and firm, have translucent flesh, and smell fresh. Signs of poor quality are an unpleasant ammonia odor and blackened edges or spots on the shells.

Florida Crab Cakes

Confused about whether the crabmeat you purchased is cooked? Relax, all crabmeat is sold cooked.

1 slightly beaten egg

½ cup fine dry bread crumbs

2 tablespoons finely chopped green onion

2 tablespoons mayonnaise or salad dressing

1 tablespoon snipped parsley

2 teaspoons snipped fresh thyme or ½ teaspoon dried thyme, crushed

2 teaspoons Dijon-style or Creole mustard

½ teaspoon white wine Worcestershire sauce

⅛ teaspoon salt

1½ cups flaked, cooked crabmeat or one 6-ounce can crabmeat, drained, flaked, and cartilage removed

¼ cup cornmeal

2 tablespoons cooking oil

Mixed salad greens (optional)

Tartar Sauce (see recipe, page 169) (optional)

Lemon wedges (optional)

In a medium bowl combine egg, ¼ cup of the bread crumbs, green onion, mayonnaise or salad dressing, parsley, thyme, mustard, Worcestershire sauce, and salt. Add crabmeat; mix well. Shape mixture into four ¾-inch-thick patties.

In a small bowl combine the remaining bread crumbs and cornmeal. Coat patties with cornmeal mixture.

In a large skillet cook crab cakes in hot oil over medium heat about 6 minutes or until crab cakes are golden and heated through, turning once (add additional oil if necessary during cooking).

If desired, serve crab cakes on a bed of mixed greens, top with Tartar Sauce, and garnish with lemon wedges. Makes 4 servings.

Nutrition information per serving: 259 calories, 13 g protein, 17 g carbohydrate, 15 g fat (2 g saturated), 100 mg cholesterol, 401 mg sodium.

𝓜USTARD MAGIC

The flavor of Florida Crab Cakes (above) takes on new dimensions depending on the mustard you use. Dijon-style mustard, made with mustard seeds, white wine, and a blend of spices, adds a clean, sharp note that complements the crab. Creole mustard, made with mustard seeds, vinegar, and horseradish, adds a hot, spicy accent.

Pan-Seared Scallops

This is a flash in the pan! Sweet scallops are given a Cajun-flavored crust, then tossed with balsamic vinegar-dressed spinach and crisp bacon. Serve with corn bread and cold beer and you have a meal that's both homey and elegant in no time flat.

1	pound fresh or frozen sea scallops
2	tablespoons all-purpose flour
1	to 2 teaspoons blackened steak seasoning or Cajun seasoning
1	tablespoon cooking oil
1	10-ounce package prewashed spinach
1	tablespoon water
2	tablespoons balsamic vinegar
¼	cup cooked bacon pieces

Thaw scallops, if frozen. Rinse scallops; pat dry with paper towels. In a plastic or paper bag combine the flour and blackened steak or Cajun seasoning. Add scallops; toss to coat.

In a 12-inch skillet cook the coated scallops in hot oil over medium heat about 6 minutes or until browned and opaque, turning once. Remove the scallops.

Add spinach to skillet; sprinkle with water. Cover and cook over medium-high heat about 2 minutes or just until spinach is wilted. Drizzle with vinegar; toss to coat evenly. Return scallops to skillet; heat through. Sprinkle with bacon. Makes 4 servings.

Nutrition information per serving: 158 calories, 18 g protein, 9 g carbohydrate, 6 g fat (1 g saturated), 37 mg cholesterol, 323 mg sodium.

Scallops in Curry Sauce

Because of their larger size, sea scallops work better than bay scallops for stir-frying. Choose scallops that are firm, sweet smelling, and free of excess cloudy liquid.

12 ounces fresh or frozen sea scallops
1 cup water
1 tablespoon cornstarch
2 teaspoons soy sauce
1 teaspoon sugar
1 tablespoon cooking oil
2 teaspoons grated gingerroot
4 cloves garlic, minced
3 stalks celery, thinly bias-sliced
2 medium carrots, thinly bias-sliced
4 ounces fresh mushrooms, quartered
    (1½ cups)
4 green onions, cut into 1-inch
    pieces (⅔ cup)
1 teaspoon curry powder
2 cups hot cooked rice
⅓ cup chutney
    Toasted Pita Wedges (see recipe,
        page 15) (optional)

Thaw scallops, if frozen. Rinse scallops; pat dry with paper towels. Cut any large scallops in half. Set aside.

For sauce, in a small bowl stir together the water, cornstarch, soy sauce, and sugar. Set aside.

Add cooking oil to a wok or large skillet. Preheat over medium-high heat (add more oil if necessary during cooking). Stir-fry the gingerroot and garlic in hot oil for 15 seconds. Add celery and carrots; stir-fry for 2 minutes. Add mushrooms and green onions; stir-fry for 1 minute. Sprinkle curry powder over vegetables. Stir-fry about 1 minute more or until vegetables are crisp-tender. Remove vegetables from wok.

Add scallops to wok. Stir-fry about 2 minutes or until scallops are opaque. Push scallops from center of wok.

Stir sauce; add to center of wok. Cook and stir until thickened and bubbly. Return cooked vegetables to wok. Gently stir all ingredients together to coat. Cook and stir for 1 to 2 minutes more or until heated through.

Serve immediately with hot cooked rice, chutney, and, if desired, Toasted Pita Wedges. Makes 4 servings.

Nutrition information per serving: 290 calories, 15 g protein, 48 g carbohydrate, 5 g fat (1 g saturated fat), 25 mg cholesterol, 359 mg sodium.

Meatless
DISHES

Contents

HERBED PASTA PRIMAVERA
(recipe, page 193)

Spicy Black Beans and Rice

Instead of rice, spoon the warm black bean mixture over squares of freshly baked corn bread.

1 medium onion, chopped (½ cup)
4 cloves garlic, minced
2 tablespoons olive oil or cooking oil
1 15-ounce can black beans, rinsed and drained
1 14½-ounce can Mexican-style stewed tomatoes
⅛ to ¼ teaspoon ground red pepper
2 cups hot cooked brown or long grain rice
¼ cup chopped onion (optional)

In a medium saucepan cook ½ cup onion and garlic in hot oil until onion is tender. Carefully stir in the drained beans, undrained tomatoes, and red pepper. Bring to boiling; reduce heat. Simmer, uncovered, for 15 minutes.

To serve, mound rice on dinner plates; make a well in the centers. Spoon black bean mixture into centers. If desired, sprinkle with ¼ cup onion. Makes 4 servings.

Nutrition information per serving: 279 calories, 11 g protein, 47 g carbohydrate, 8 g fat (1 g saturated), 0 mg cholesterol, 631 mg sodium.

Warm Beans with Herbed Tomatoes And Goat Cheese

Get extra mileage out of this recipe by chilling any leftovers and serving them as salad with warm tortillas.

3 medium ripe tomatoes, seeded and chopped (2 cups)
¼ cup snipped fresh basil
¼ cup snipped fresh oregano
2 green onions, sliced
1 clove garlic, minced
½ teaspoon salt
¼ teaspoon pepper
1 15-ounce can small red beans or kidney beans
1 15-ounce can Great Northern beans or navy beans
4 ounces semisoft goat (chèvre) cheese or feta cheese, crumbled (1 cup)

In a medium bowl combine chopped tomatoes, basil, oregano, green onions, garlic, salt, and pepper. Let stand at room temperature for 30 minutes to 2 hours.

In a medium saucepan combine undrained red or kidney beans and undrained Great Northern or navy beans. Bring to boiling; reduce heat. Cover and simmer about 2 minutes or until mixture is heated through. Drain.

To serve, toss warm beans with tomato mixture. Sprinkle with cheese. Serve warm. Makes 4 servings.

Nutrition information per serving: 304 calories, 22 g protein, 45 g carbohydrate, 7 g fat (4 g saturated), 13 mg cholesterol, 558 mg sodium.

Spicy Black Beans and Rice

Cheese Tortellini with Cannellini Bean Sauce

You can make this low-fat pasta dish in a snap thanks to refrigerated tortellini and canned beans. Try it for a busy weeknight dinner with crusty sourdough bread and fresh fruit.

1   9-ounce package refrigerated
    cheese-stuffed tortellini
1   15-ounce can white kidney
    (cannellini) beans, rinsed and
    drained
⅔   cup milk
⅔   cup thin slivers of red, yellow,
    and/or green sweet pepper
¼   cup grated Parmesan cheese
1   tablespoon snipped fresh oregano or
    1 teaspoon dried oregano, crushed
¼   teaspoon salt
¼   teaspoon ground nutmeg
⅛   teaspoon black pepper
    Finely shredded Parmesan cheese
    (optional)
    Fresh oregano sprigs (optional)

Cook the pasta according to package directions. Drain; keep warm.

Meanwhile, for sauce, in a food processor bowl or blender container combine the beans and milk. Cover and process or blend until smooth. Transfer the bean mixture to a large skillet.

Stir in sweet pepper slivers, grated Parmesan cheese, snipped fresh or dried oregano, salt, nutmeg, and black pepper. Cook and stir until mixture is heated through.

Arrange the cooked pasta on dinner plates or a large platter. Spoon the sauce over pasta.

If desired, sprinkle each serving with finely shredded Parmesan cheese and garnish with fresh oregano sprigs. Makes 4 servings.

Nutrition information per serving: 304 calories, 21 g protein, 48 g carbohydrate, 6 g fat (2 g saturated), 43 mg cholesterol, 730 mg sodium.

*B*EYOND RED KIDNEY BEANS

When you think of kidney beans, the red ones probably come to mind. But their Italian cousins, the cannellini beans, also are a versatile and delicious choice. These white, mild-tasting beans are ideal for making casseroles, soups, stews, and other one-dish meals, such as Cheese Tortellini with Cannellini Bean Sauce (above). Cannellini come in both canned and dried forms. Look for them with the other canned or dried beans in your supermarket or at Italian food specialty stores.

Four Bean Enchiladas

We chose kidney, garbanzo, pinto, and navy or Great Northern beans to make this tasty crowd-size recipe, but you can use any combination of beans that you like.

16 6-inch corn tortillas
 1 15-ounce can red kidney beans, rinsed and drained
 1 15-ounce can garbanzo beans, rinsed and drained
 1 15-ounce can pinto beans, rinsed and drained
 1 15-ounce can navy or Great Northern beans, rinsed and drained
 1 11-ounce can condensed cheddar cheese or nacho cheese soup
 1 10-ounce can enchilada sauce
 1 8-ounce can tomato sauce
 1½ cups shredded Monterey Jack or cheddar cheese (6 ounces)
     Sliced pitted ripe olives (optional)
     Green sweet pepper strips (optional)

Wrap corn tortillas in foil and bake in a 350° oven about 10 minutes or until tortillas are warm.

For filling, in a large mixing bowl combine beans and cheese soup. Spoon about ⅓ cup filling onto one end of each tortilla. Starting from the end with the filling, roll up each tortilla.

Arrange tortillas, seam sides down, in 2 ungreased 2-quart rectangular baking dishes or 8 individual au gratin dishes.

In a medium mixing bowl stir together the enchilada sauce and tomato sauce. Pour over tortillas.

Cover and bake in the 350° oven about 30 minutes for baking dishes (about 20 minutes for au gratin dishes) or until heated through. Sprinkle with shredded cheese.

Bake, uncovered, about 5 minutes more or until cheese is melted. If desired, sprinkle the enchiladas with ripe olives and green pepper strips. Makes 8 servings.

Nutrition information per serving: 491 calories, 25 g protein, 71 g carbohydrate, 14 g fat (7 g saturated), 29 mg cholesterol, 1,599 mg sodium.

Savory Shepherd's Pie

To speed preparation, substitute packaged instant mashed potatoes (enough for 4 servings) for the 3 small potatoes and stir the garlic mixture into the prepared instant potatoes.

3	small potatoes (12 ounces)
2	cloves garlic, minced
½	teaspoon dried basil, crushed
2	tablespoons margarine or butter
¼	teaspoon salt
2	to 4 tablespoons milk
1	medium onion, chopped
1	medium carrot, sliced
1	tablespoon cooking oil
1	15-ounce can kidney beans, rinsed and drained
1	14½-ounce can tomatoes, drained and cut up
1	10-ounce package frozen mixed vegetables or whole kernel corn
1	8-ounce can tomato sauce
1	teaspoon Worcestershire sauce
½	teaspoon sugar
1	cup shredded cheddar cheese
	Paprika (optional)

Peel and quarter potatoes. In a covered large saucepan cook potatoes in a small amount of boiling, lightly salted water for 20 to 25 minutes or until tender. Drain.

Mash with a potato masher or beat with an electric mixer on low speed. In a small saucepan cook garlic and basil in margarine or butter for 15 seconds. Add to mashed potatoes along with salt. Gradually beat in enough of the milk to make light and fluffy. Set aside.

For filling, in a medium saucepan cook onion and carrot in hot oil until onion is tender. Stir in beans, tomatoes, frozen vegetables, tomato sauce, Worcestershire sauce, and sugar. Heat until mixture is bubbly.

Transfer filling to an ungreased 8x8x2-inch baking pan. Drop mashed potatoes in 4 mounds over filling. Sprinkle with cheddar cheese and, if desired, paprika. Bake in a 375° oven for 25 to 30 minutes or until heated through and cheese starts to brown. Makes 4 servings.

Nutrition information per serving: 456 calories, 20 g protein, 60 g carbohydrate, 19 g fat (8 g saturated), 31 mg cholesterol, 1,130 mg sodium.

Herbed Pasta Primavera

For the best flavor, use fresh parsley, fresh basil, and freshly shredded Parmesan cheese.

6 ounces packaged dried linguine, spaghetti, or fettuccine
1 cup water
2 teaspoons cornstarch
2 teaspoons instant vegetable or chicken bouillon granules
1 tablespoon olive oil
2 cloves garlic, minced
8 ounces asparagus, cut into 1-inch pieces
2 medium carrots, thinly bias-sliced
1 medium onion, chopped
1 6-ounce package frozen pea pods, thawed and well drained
⅔ cup sliced almonds
¼ cup snipped parsley
1½ teaspoons dried basil, crushed
¼ teaspoon pepper
⅓ cup finely shredded Parmesan cheese

Cook pasta according to package directions. Drain; keep warm. Meanwhile, for sauce, in a small bowl stir together the water, cornstarch, and vegetable or chicken bouillon granules. Set aside.

Add olive oil to a wok or large skillet. Preheat over medium-high heat. Stir-fry garlic in hot oil for 15 seconds. Add asparagus, carrots, and onion; stir fry for 2 minutes. Add pea pods, nuts, parsley, basil, and pepper. Stir-fry about 1 minute more or until vegetables are crisp-tender. Remove vegetable mixture from wok.

Stir sauce; add to wok. Cook and stir until thickened and bubbly. Cook and stir for 1 minute more. Return vegetable mixture to wok. Cook and stir until heated through. Serve immediately over pasta. Sprinkle with Parmesan cheese. Makes 4 servings.

Nutrition information per serving: 432 calories, 17 g protein, 52 g carbohydrate, 19 g fat (3 g saturated), 7 mg cholesterol, 642 mg sodium.

Vegetable Lasagna

In a hurry? Substitute 2 cups of prepared spaghetti sauce for the Red Pepper Sauce in this recipe.

6 no-boil lasagna noodles or regular
   lasagna noodles
8 ounces zucchini and/or yellow
   summer squash, halved
   lengthwise and sliced
2 cups sliced fresh mushrooms
⅓ cup chopped onion
2 teaspoons olive oil
1 cup fat-free or low-fat ricotta cheese
¼ cup finely shredded Parmesan cheese
¼ teaspoon black pepper
   Red Pepper Sauce
1 cup shredded part-skim mozzarella
   cheese (4 ounces)
1 medium tomato, seeded and
   chopped
   Fresh oregano sprigs (optional)

Soak the no-boil lasagna noodles in warm water for 10 minutes. (Or, cook regular noodles according to package directions, except omit salt.) Drain.

Meanwhile, in a large skillet cook zucchini and/or yellow squash, mushrooms, and onion in hot olive oil about 6 minutes or until squash is tender, stirring occasionally. Drain well.

In a small bowl stir together ricotta cheese, Parmesan cheese, and black pepper. To assemble, place 3 lasagna noodles in a 2-quart square baking dish, trimming to fit as necessary. Top with ricotta mixture, half of the vegetable mixture, half of the Red Pepper Sauce, and half of the mozzarella cheese. Layer with the remaining lasagna noodles, vegetable mixture, and sauce.

Bake in a 375° oven for 30 minutes. Sprinkle with remaining mozzarella cheese and the tomato. Bake about 5 minutes more or until heated through. Let stand for 10 minutes before serving. If desired, garnish with oregano sprigs. Makes 6 servings.

Red Pepper Sauce: In a large skillet cook 3 cups chopped *red sweet pepper* and 4 whole cloves *garlic* in 1 tablespoon *olive oil* or *cooking oil* over medium heat for 20 minutes, stirring occasionally. (Or, use one 12-ounce jar *roasted red sweet peppers,* drained. Omit cooking step.) Place mixture in a blender container. Cover and blend until nearly smooth. Add ½ cup *water,* ¼ cup *tomato paste,* 2 tablespoons *red wine vinegar,* and 1 tablespoon snipped *fresh oregano* or ½ teaspoon *dried oregano,* crushed. Cover and blend just until nearly smooth. Return to skillet; heat through. Makes 2 cups.

Nutrition information per serving: 249 calories, 17 g protein, 28 g carbohydrate, 9 g fat (3 g saturated), 18 mg cholesterol, 292 mg sodium.

Tofu and Cheese-Stuffed Shells

No one will ever know that these giant pasta shells contain tofu ... unless you tell.

12 packaged dried jumbo pasta shells
¼ cup shredded carrot
1 green onion, sliced
8 ounces tofu (fresh bean curd), drained
½ cup ricotta cheese
½ cup shredded cheddar cheese
½ cup shredded mozzarella cheese
1 egg white
¼ teaspoon salt
¼ teaspoon pepper
1 14½-ounce can tomatoes, cut up
½ of a 6-ounce can (⅓ cup) tomato paste
1 teaspoon dried basil, crushed
1 teaspoon dried oregano, crushed
½ teaspoon sugar
¼ teaspoon garlic powder
¼ teaspoon fennel seed, crushed (optional)
Grated Parmesan cheese (optional)

Cook pasta according to package directions. Drain pasta; rinse with cold water. Drain again.

Meanwhile, in a small saucepan cook carrot and green onion in a small amount of water until tender. Drain.

For filling, in a medium mixing bowl mash tofu with a fork. Stir in carrot mixture, ricotta cheese, cheddar cheese, ¼ cup of the mozzarella cheese, egg white, salt, and pepper. Set aside.

For sauce, in a medium saucepan combine the undrained cut-up tomatoes, tomato paste, basil, oregano, sugar, garlic powder, and, if desired, fennel seed. Bring to boiling; reduce heat. Simmer, uncovered, for 10 minutes.

To assemble, stuff each pasta shell with about 1 rounded tablespoon filling. Place in an ungreased 2-quart square baking dish. Pour the sauce over stuffed pasta shells.

Cover and bake in a 350° oven about 25 minutes or until heated through. Sprinkle with the remaining mozzarella cheese. If desired, serve with Parmesan cheese. Makes 4 servings.

Nutrition information per serving: 318 calories, 21 g protein, 32 g carbohydrate, 13 g fat (6 g saturated), 32 mg cholesterol, 558 mg sodium.

Pasta Rosa-Verde

This red, white, and green dish on the table will make any flag-waving Italian feel patriotic (not to mention famished)! Fresh tomatoes are quick-cooked with peppery arugula and topped with tangy Gorgonzola cheese.

8	ounces packaged dried cut ziti or mostaccioli
1	medium onion, thinly sliced
2	cloves garlic, minced
1	tablespoon olive oil
4	to 6 medium tomatoes, seeded and coarsely chopped
1	teaspoon salt
½	teaspoon freshly ground black pepper
¼	teaspoon crushed red pepper (optional)
3	cups arugula, watercress, and/or spinach, coarsely chopped
¼	cup pine nuts or slivered almonds, toasted
2	tablespoons crumbled Gorgonzola or other blue cheese

Cook pasta according to package directions. Drain; keep warm.

Meanwhile, for sauce, in a large skillet cook the onion and garlic in hot olive oil over medium heat until onion is tender.

Add tomatoes, salt, black pepper, and, if desired, red pepper. Cook and stir over medium-high heat about 2 minutes or until the tomatoes are warm and release some of their juices. Stir in arugula, watercress, and/or spinach. Heat just until greens are wilted.

Arrange the pasta in individual serving bowls. Spoon the sauce over the pasta. Sprinkle with toasted pine nuts or almonds and Gorgonzola or other blue cheese. Makes 4 servings.

Nutrition information per serving: 352 calories, 12 g protein, 54 g carbohydrate, 11 g fat (2 g saturated), 3 mg cholesterol, 610 mg sodium.

ALL ABOUT ARUGULA

Arugula, sometimes called rocket, is a peppery, pungent salad green that adds a spicy flavor to dishes. Select arugula with fresh, small, rich green leaves. Avoid yellowed or wilted leaves. When you bring arugula home, refrigerate it in a plastic bag for up to 2 days. To use it, gently wash the leaves by immersing them in cold water until there is no trace of grit and sand. Pat the arugula leaves dry with paper towels.

Gingered Vegetable-Tofu Stir-Fry

Buy extra-firm tofu to prevent it from breaking apart while stir-frying this flavorful dish.

1 cup water
¼ cup dry sherry or dry white wine
2 tablespoons soy sauce
4 teaspoons cornstarch
½ teaspoon sugar
1 tablespoon cooking oil
2 teaspoons grated gingerroot
1 pound asparagus, cut into 1-inch pieces (3 cups), or one 10-ounce package frozen cut asparagus, thawed and well drained
1 small yellow summer squash, halved lengthwise and sliced (1¼ cups)
2 green onions, sliced
1 10½-ounce package extra-firm tofu (fresh bean curd), cut into ½-inch cubes
½ cup pine nuts or chopped almonds, toasted
2 cups hot cooked brown rice

For sauce, in a small bowl stir together water, sherry or wine, soy sauce, cornstarch, and sugar. Set aside.

Add cooking oil to a wok or large skillet. Preheat over medium-high heat (add more oil if necessary during cooking). Stir-fry gingerroot in hot oil for 15 seconds. Add fresh asparagus (if using) and squash; stir-fry for 3 minutes. Add thawed asparagus (if using) and green onions; stir-fry about 1½ minutes more or until asparagus is crisp-tender. Remove from wok.

Add tofu to wok. Gently stir-fry for 2 to 3 minutes or until lightly browned. Remove from wok. Stir sauce; add to wok. Cook and stir until thickened and bubbly.

Return cooked vegetables and tofu to wok. Gently stir all ingredients together to coat. Cover and cook about 1 minute more or until heated through. Stir in toasted pine nuts or almonds. Serve immediately over hot cooked brown rice. Makes 4 servings.

Nutrition information per serving: 412 calories, 22 g protein, 38 g carbohydrate, 21 g fat (3 g saturated), 0 mg cholesterol, 541 mg sodium.

TOFU TIPS

Tofu is soybean curd that's made from soybean milk by a process similar to the one used for making cheese. It's sold in blocks or cakes and comes in soft, firm, and extra-firm styles. Extra-firm tofu is good for stir-fried dishes because it holds its shape well. Look for it in the refrigerated area of your supermarket produce section.

Mu Shu Vegetable Roll-Ups

Instead of wrapping up our Mu Shu vegetables in the traditional Peking pancakes, we went Mexican and used ready-made flour tortillas. For easier handling, be sure to warm the tortillas before filling.

2 tablespoons water
2 tablespoons soy sauce
½ teaspoon sugar
½ teaspoon cornstarch
8 to 10 8-inch flour tortillas
1 tablespoon cooking oil
1 teaspoon grated gingerroot
2 cloves garlic, minced
2 medium carrots, cut into julienne
   strips
½ of a small head cabbage, shredded
   (3 cups)
1 medium zucchini, cut into julienne
   strips (1¼ cups)
4 cups sliced fresh mushrooms
2 cups fresh bean sprouts
½ of a medium jicama, peeled and cut
   into julienne strips (1 cup)
8 ounces firm tofu (bean curd), well
   drained and cut into ¾-inch cubes
8 green onions, sliced (1 cup)
¼ cup hoisin sauce
   Cherry tomato flowers (optional)
   Green onion brushes (optional)

For sauce, in a small bowl stir together water, soy sauce, sugar, and cornstarch. Set aside.

Wrap tortillas in foil and bake in a 350° oven about 10 minutes or until warm. [Or, just before serving, microwave tortillas, covered, on 100% power (high) about 1 minute or until warm.]

Meanwhile, pour cooking oil into a wok or large skillet. Preheat over medium-high heat (add more oil if necessary during cooking). Stir-fry gingerroot and garlic in hot oil for 15 seconds. Add carrot strips; stir-fry for 1 minute. Add cabbage and zucchini; stir-fry for 1 minute. Add mushrooms, bean sprouts, and jicama strips. Stir-fry for 1 to 2 minutes more or until vegetables are crisp-tender. Push vegetables from center of wok.

Stir sauce; add to center of wok. Cook and stir until thickened and bubbly. Add tofu and sliced green onions. Gently stir all ingredients together to coat. Cover and cook about 2 minutes more or until mixture is heated through.

Spread warm tortillas with hoisin sauce. Spoon the vegetable mixture onto each tortilla. Fold over one side of tortilla to cover some of the filling. Then fold the two adjacent sides of tortilla over filling. Secure with toothpicks, if necessary. If desired, garnish with tomato flowers and green onion brushes. Serve immediately. Makes 4 or 5 servings.

Nutrition information per serving: 399 calories, 20 g protein, 57 g carbohydrate, 12 g fat (2 g saturated fat), 0 mg cholesterol, 1,811 mg sodium.

South-of-the-Border Pie

Kidney beans, brown rice, eggs, and cheddar cheese provide the protein while chili powder and cumin provide the kick. Serve this Mexican-style dish with a simple tossed salad.

1   medium onion, chopped
2   cloves garlic, minced
1   tablespoon olive oil or cooking oil
1   to 2 teaspoons chili powder
1   teaspoon ground cumin
¼   teaspoon salt
1   15-ounce can red kidney beans,
    rinsed and drained
1½ cups cooked brown rice
1   cup shredded cheddar cheese
    (4 ounces)
¾   cup milk
2   slightly beaten eggs
    Green sweet pepper strips (optional)
    Salsa (optional)

Lightly grease a 10-inch quiche dish or pie plate. Set aside. In a large saucepan cook onion and garlic in hot oil until tender. Stir in chili powder, cumin, and salt. Cook and stir for 1 minute more. Cool. Stir in beans, cooked brown rice, cheese, milk, and eggs.

Spoon the bean mixture into the prepared baking dish. Bake in a 350° oven about 25 minutes or until the center is set. Let stand for 10 minutes. If desired, sprinkle the pie with green pepper strips and serve with salsa. Makes 6 servings.

Nutrition information per serving: 254 calories, 14 g protein, 26 g carbohydrate, 12 g fat (5 g saturated), 93 mg cholesterol, 366 mg sodium.

SODIUM SENSE FOR BEANS

Using canned beans in recipes can save you time, but they also can contribute sodium to your diet. A simple solution to this salty situation is to rinse the beans in a colander under running water and let them drain. You'll still have great tasting beans without the salty liquid that comes with them.

Southern Grits Casserole with Red Pepper Relish

To make a roasted pepper relish, substitute one 12-ounce jar roasted red sweet peppers for the fresh sweet peppers. Drain and chop the roasted peppers and stir into the cooked onion mixture.

4   cups water
1   cup quick-cooking grits
4   slightly beaten eggs
2   cups shredded cheddar cheese
      (8 ounces)
½   cup milk
¼   cup sliced green onions
1   to 2 jalapeño peppers, seeded
      (if desired) and chopped
½   teaspoon garlic salt
¼   teaspoon white pepper
      Sliced green onions (optional)
2   medium red sweet peppers, chopped
      (2 cups)
1   small red onion, chopped (½ cup)
2   cloves garlic, minced
1   tablespoon margarine or butter
⅓   cup snipped parsley
1   tablespoon white wine vinegar

In a large saucepan bring water to boiling. Slowly stir in grits. Gradually stir about 1 cup of the hot mixture into the eggs. Return to saucepan. Remove from heat.

Stir the shredded cheese, milk, ¼ cup green onions, jalapeño peppers, garlic salt, and white pepper into the grits mixture.

Spoon the grits mixture into an ungreased 2-quart casserole. Bake in a 350° oven for 45 to 50 minutes or until a knife inserted near center comes out clean If desired, sprinkle with additional green onions.

Meanwhile, for relish, in a medium saucepan cook the red sweet peppers, red onion, and garlic in margarine or butter just until peppers are tender. Remove from heat. Stir in parsley and vinegar.

Let relish stand at room temperature at least 30 minutes. Serve the relish with grits. Makes 4 servings.

Nutrition information per serving: 403 calories, 23 g protein, 16 g carbohydrate, 27 g fat (14 g saturated), 275 mg cholesterol, 731 mg sodium.

Fresh Vegetable Risotto

Classic risotto is an Italian specialty made by simmering and constantly stirring rice so it slowly absorbs the cooking liquid, resulting in a creamy dish. This one is flavored with colorful vegetables and two cheeses.

2 cups sliced fresh mushrooms
1 medium onion, chopped
2 cloves garlic, minced
2 tablespoons olive oil or cooking oil
1 cup Arborio or long grain rice
3 cups vegetable or chicken broth
¾ cup bite-size asparagus or broccoli pieces
1 medium tomato, seeded and chopped (⅔ cup)
¼ cup shredded carrot
1 cup shredded fontina or Muenster cheese (4 ounces)
¼ cup grated Parmesan cheese
3 tablespoons snipped fresh basil or parsley
  Tomato slices (optional)

In a large saucepan cook the mushrooms, onion, and garlic in hot oil until onion is tender. Stir in uncooked Arborio or long grain rice. Cook and stir for 5 minutes.

Meanwhile, in another saucepan bring the vegetable or chicken broth to boiling; reduce heat and simmer. Slowly add 1 cup of the broth to rice mixture, stirring constantly. Continue to cook and stir rice mixture over medium heat until liquid is absorbed.

Add another ½ cup of the broth and the asparagus or broccoli to rice mixture, stirring constantly. Continue to cook and stir until the liquid is absorbed. Add another 1 cup broth, ½ cup at a time, stirring constantly until the liquid is absorbed. (This should take about 15 minutes.)

Stir in the chopped tomato, carrot, and the remaining ½ cup broth. Cook and stir until rice is slightly creamy and just tender.

Stir in fontina or Muenster cheese, Parmesan cheese, and basil or parsley. If desired, garnish with tomato slices. Serve immediately. Makes 4 servings.

Nutrition information per serving: 401 calories, 15 g protein, 47 g carbohydrate, 19 g fat (8 g saturated), 38 mg cholesterol, 1,052 mg sodium.

Vegetarian Fried Rice

Transform fried rice from a side dish into a sumptuous meal by adding extra eggs and lots of vegetables.

5   slightly beaten eggs
1   tablespoon soy sauce
2   tablespoons cooking oil
1   small onion, chopped (⅓ cup)
1   clove garlic, minced
2   stalks celery, thinly bias-sliced
       (1 cup)
1½ cups sliced fresh mushrooms
1   medium green sweet pepper,
       chopped (¾ cup)
4   cups cold cooked rice
1   8-ounce can bamboo shoots,
       drained
2   medium carrots, shredded (1 cup)
¾   cup frozen peas, thawed
3   tablespoons soy sauce
3   green onions, sliced (⅓ cup)
     Crinkle-cut carrot slices (optional)

In a small bowl combine eggs and 1 tablespoon soy sauce. Set aside.

Add 1 tablespoon of the cooking oil to a wok or large skillet. Preheat over medium heat. Stir-fry chopped onion and garlic in hot oil about 2 minutes or until crisp-tender.

Add the egg mixture to wok and stir gently to scramble. When eggs are set, remove from wok. Cut up any large pieces of egg mixture. Let wok cool slightly.

Add remaining oil to cooled wok. Preheat over medium-high heat (add more oil if necessary during cooking). Stir-fry celery in hot oil for 1 minute. Add the mushrooms and green pepper; stir-fry for 1 to 2 minutes more or until vegetables are crisp-tender.

Add cooked rice, bamboo shoots, shredded carrots, and peas. Sprinkle with 3 tablespoons soy sauce. Cook and stir for 4 to 6 minutes or until heated through. Add the cooked egg mixture and green onions. Cook and stir about 1 minute more or until heated through.

If desired, garnish fried rice with carrot slices. Serve immediately. Makes 4 or 5 servings.

Nutrition information per serving: 438 calories, 17 g protein, 61 g carbohydrate, 14 g fat (3 g saturated fat), 266 mg cholesterol, 1,177 mg sodium.

Fresh Tomato Pizza with Pesto

For best results, make this recipe when ripe, juicy summer tomatoes are at their peak.

½ cup pesto
1 12-inch Italian bread shell (Boboli)
3 medium ripe tomatoes, thinly sliced
1 2¼-ounce can sliced pitted ripe
   olives, drained (scant ⅔ cup)
   Freshly ground pepper
2 cups shredded Monterey Jack or
   mozzarella cheese (8 ounces)

Spread pesto evenly over bread shell. Place on large pizza pan or baking sheet. Top with tomato slices. Sprinkle with olives and pepper. Top with Monterey Jack or mozzarella cheese.

Bake in a 425° oven for 10 to 15 minutes or until cheese is melted and tomatoes are warm. Cut into wedges. Makes 4 servings.

Nutrition information per serving: 776 calories, 32 g protein, 60 g carbohydrate, 48 g fat (11 g saturated), 60 mg cholesterol, 1,265 mg sodium.

Double Corn Tortilla Casserole

The double dose of corn comes from corn tortillas and whole kernel corn. Serve this tangy home-style dish with your favorite salsa or picante sauce.

8 6-inch corn tortillas
1½ cups shredded Monterey Jack cheese
   (6 ounces)
1 cup frozen whole kernel corn
4 green onions, sliced
2 slightly beaten eggs
1 cup buttermilk
1 4-ounce can diced green chile
   peppers

Grease a 2-quart square baking dish. Tear tortillas into bite-size pieces. Arrange half of the tortillas in prepared baking dish. Top with half of the cheese, half of the corn, and half of the green onions. Layer with the remaining tortillas, cheese, corn, and green onions.

In a medium mixing bowl stir together the eggs, buttermilk, and undrained chile peppers. Gently pour over tortilla mixture. Bake in a 325° oven about 30 minutes or until a knife inserted near the center comes out clean. Serve warm. Makes 4 servings.

Nutrition information per serving: 388 calories, 21 g protein, 37 g carbohydrate, 18 g fat (9 g saturated), 146 mg cholesterol, 564 mg sodium.

Fresh Tomato Pizza with Pesto

Curried Vegetable Stir-Fry

This flavorful vegetable entrée fuses Asian stir-frying with curry and European Brussels sprouts.

2   cups water
1¼ cups quick-cooking pearl barley
1   cup fresh Brussels sprouts, halved,
      or frozen Brussels sprouts, thawed
      and halved
1   cup cold water
4   teaspoons cornstarch
1   to 2 teaspoons curry powder
1   teaspoon instant vegetable bouillon
      granules
    Nonstick spray coating
2   medium red, yellow, and/or green
      sweet peppers, cut into bite-size
      strips (1½ cups)
2   tablespoons thinly sliced green
      onion
1   cup bias-sliced carrots
¼   cup peanuts

Bring 2 cups water to boiling. Stir in barley. Return to boiling; reduce heat. Simmer, covered, for 10 to 12 minutes or until tender. If necessary, drain. Cook Brussels sprouts in a small amount of boiling water for 3 minutes. Drain. For sauce, stir together 1 cup water, cornstarch, curry powder, and bouillon granules.

Spray an unheated wok or large skillet with nonstick coating. Preheat over medium-high heat. Stir-fry the peppers and green onion in hot wok for 1 minute. Add the Brussels sprouts and carrots; stir-fry for 3 minutes. Push from center of wok. Stir sauce; add to center of wok. Cook and stir until thickened and bubbly. Stir all ingredients together to coat. Cook and stir for 2 minutes more. Serve immediately over barley. Sprinkle with peanuts. Makes 4 servings.

Nutrition information per serving: 320 calories, 10 g protein, 59 g carbohydrate, 6 g fat (1 g saturated fat), 0 mg cholesterol, 333 mg sodium.

BIAS-SLICING

To bias-slice vegetables, such as carrots or green onions, or meats, hold a sharp knife at a 45-degree angle to the vegetable or meat and cut into thin diagonal slices. Partially freezing the meat before bias-slicing makes it easier to cut thin slices.

Spaghetti Squash Italiano

Spaghetti squash is a tasty, low-calorie, high-vitamin substitute for spaghetti.

2 small spaghetti squash (1¼ to
   1½ pounds each)
4 ounces mozzarella cheese, cut into
   small cubes (1 cup)
3 medium tomatoes, seeded and
   chopped (2 cups)
4 green onions, sliced
½ cup pine nuts or coarsely chopped
   walnuts, toasted
¼ cup snipped fresh basil or parsley
1 tablespoon olive oil or cooking oil
2 cloves garlic, minced
2 tablespoons grated Parmesan cheese

Halve the squash lengthwise and remove the seeds. Prick skin all over with a sharp knife. Place halves, cut sides down, in a 3-quart rectangular baking dish. Cover and bake in a 350° oven for 60 to 70 minutes or until squash is tender.

Using a fork, carefully rake the squash pulp to separate it into strands, leaving the strands in the shells. Sprinkle one-fourth of the mozzarella cheese over each shell; toss lightly. Push the squash mixture up the sides of the shells.

Meanwhile, for filling, in a medium mixing bowl combine tomatoes, green onions, nuts, basil or parsley, oil, and garlic. Spoon the filling into squash shells. Sprinkle with Parmesan cheese.

Return to baking dish. Bake about 20 minutes more or until filling is heated through. Makes 4 servings.

Nutrition information per serving: 304 calories, 15 g protein, 23 g carbohydrate, 20 g fat (6 g saturated), 18 mg cholesterol, 237 mg sodium.

QUICK-COOKING SPAGHETTI SQUASH

Save time by cooking spaghetti squash in your microwave oven. Prick whole squash with a sharp knife. Place squash in a microwave-safe baking dish. Micro-cook, uncovered, on 100% power (high) for 15 to 20 minutes or until tender. Let stand for 5 minutes. Halve squash lengthwise and remove seeds.

Crispy Eggplant with Tomato-Feta Cheese Sauce

For a mild cheese flavor, sprinkle feta cheese over the spaghetti sauce. For a more robust cheese flavor, use blue cheese.

1 medium eggplant (about 1 pound), peeled and thinly sliced
2 slightly beaten eggs
2 tablespoons milk
½ cup grated Parmesan cheese
½ cup toasted wheat germ
1 teaspoon dried basil, crushed
¼ teaspoon black pepper
2 cups meatless spaghetti sauce
¼ to ½ teaspoon ground red pepper
1 cup crumbled feta or blue cheese
Snipped fresh basil (optional)

Place eggplant slices on a baking sheet. Sprinkle lightly with salt. Let stand for 10 minutes. Pat eggplant dry with paper towels.

Grease a baking sheet. Set aside. In a shallow bowl combine the eggs and milk. In another shallow bowl stir together the Parmesan cheese, wheat germ, dried basil, and black pepper.

Dip the eggplant slices in egg mixture, then into wheat germ mixture, turning to coat both sides. Place the coated slices in a single layer on prepared baking sheet.

Bake in a 400° oven for 15 to 20 minutes or until the eggplant is crisp on outside and tender on inside.

Meanwhile, for sauce, in a medium saucepan combine the spaghetti sauce and ground red pepper. Cook over medium heat until mixture is heated through.

To serve, divide the eggplant slices among dinner plates. Spoon the sauce over eggplant. Sprinkle with feta or blue cheese and, if desired, snipped fresh basil. Makes 4 servings.

Nutrition information per serving: 388 calories, 20 g protein, 35 g carbohydrate, 20 g fat (9 g saturated), 142 mg cholesterol, 1,471 mg sodium.

Sautéed Onion & Tomato Sandwiches

When laps double as the dining table, the best TV dinner is something easy and out-of-hand. This hearty whole-grain sandwich serves perfectly. Pass around beer, brownies, and your biggest napkins.

2   medium onions, sliced
1   teaspoon olive oil
8   slices hearty whole grain bread
      (toasted, if desired)
      Honey mustard
4   lettuce leaves, shredded
3   small red and/or yellow tomatoes,
      thinly sliced
      Small fresh basil leaves
4   ounces spreadable Brie cheese or
      ½ of an 8-ounce tub cream cheese

In a large skillet cook the onion slices in hot olive oil over medium-high heat for 5 to 7 minutes or until tender and just starting to brown. Remove from heat. Cool onions slightly.

To assemble, lightly spread half of the bread slices with honey mustard. Top with shredded lettuce, cooked onion slices, and tomato slices. Sprinkle with basil leaves.

Spread the remaining bread slices with Brie or cream cheese. Place on top of sandwiches. Makes 4 servings.

Nutrition information per serving: 287 calories, 12 g protein, 35 g carbohydrate, 12 g fat (6 g saturated), 28 mg cholesterol, 490 mg sodium.

Cheese and Veggie Sandwiches

If you're watching your sodium intake, you can reduce the salt in the cottage cheese by placing it in a colander and rinsing under cold water.

1½   cups cottage cheese, drained
¼   cup shredded carrot
¼   cup chopped celery or green sweet
      pepper
½   teaspoon finely snipped fresh chives
¼   cup plain low-fat yogurt
8   small slices whole grain bread
2   tablespoons horseradish mustard
      Spinach or lettuce leaves
4   tomato slices

In a medium bowl combine the cottage cheese, carrot, celery or green pepper, and chives. Stir in the yogurt.

Spread the whole grain bread slices with horseradish mustard. Place the spinach or lettuce leaves on half of the bread slices. Top with the cottage cheese mixture, tomato slices, and the remaining bread slices. Makes 4 servings.

Nutrition information per serving: 232 calories, 16 g protein, 29 g carbohydrate, 7 g fat (3 g saturated), 13 mg cholesterol, 722 mg sodium.

Sautéed Onion & Tomato Sandwiches

Cookies & CAKES

Contents

CITRUS-HAZELNUT BARS
(recipe, page 229)

Triple-Chocolate Chunk Cookies

For the true chocoholic, there is no such thing as too much chocolate. These chunky, oversize treats contain a trio of chocolates.

1 cup butter
¾ cup granulated sugar
¾ cup packed brown sugar
1 teaspoon baking soda
2 eggs
1 teaspoon vanilla
3 ounces unsweetened chocolate, melted and cooled
2 cups all-purpose flour
8 ounces semisweet chocolate, cut into ½-inch pieces, or 1⅓ cups large semisweet chocolate pieces
6 ounces white baking bar, cut into ½-inch pieces, or 1 cup white baking pieces
1 cup chopped black walnuts or pecans (optional)

Lightly grease a cookie sheet; set aside. In a large mixing bowl beat the butter with an electric mixer on medium to high speed for 30 seconds.

Add the granulated sugar, brown sugar, and baking soda; beat until combined. Beat in eggs and vanilla until combined. Stir in melted chocolate. Beat in as much of the flour as you can with the mixer. Stir in any remaining flour with a wooden spoon. Stir in the chocolate and white baking pieces and, if desired, nuts.

Drop dough by a ¼-cup dry measure or a scoop about 4 inches apart onto the prepared cookie sheet.

Bake in a 350° oven for 12 to 14 minutes or until edges are firm. Cool on cookie sheet for 1 minute. Transfer the cookies to a wire rack; cool. Makes about 22 cookies.

Nutrition information per cookie: 280 calories, 3 g protein, 33 g carbohydrate, 17 g fat (10 g saturated), 44 mg cholesterol, 158 mg sodium.

DROP COOKIE HINTS

For attractive standard-size drop cookies, use a spoon from your flatware set—not a measuring spoon—to drop them, keeping the mounds the same size and spacing them evenly on the cookie sheet. Don't crowd the mounds. When a recipe calls for a greased cookie sheet, use only a light coating of shortening. A heavy coating will cause the cookies to spread too much. Also, don't drop the dough onto a hot cookie sheet. The heat will cause the cookies to flatten. Instead, use two sheets or cool one sheet between batches.

Oatmeal Jumbos

Make these cookies large or small. Both sizes are big in peanut butter and chocolate taste.

1	cup peanut butter
½	cup butter
1½	cups packed brown sugar
½	cup granulated sugar
1½	teaspoons baking powder
½	teaspoon baking soda
3	eggs
2	teaspoons vanilla
4	cups rolled oats
1½	cups candy-coated milk chocolate pieces
¾	cup chopped peanuts, walnuts, or pecans

In a large mixing bowl beat peanut butter and butter with an electric mixer on medium to high speed for 30 seconds. Add the brown sugar, granulated sugar, baking powder, and soda; beat until combined.

Beat in the eggs and vanilla until combined. Stir in the rolled oats. Stir in the candy-coated milk chocolate pieces and nuts.

Drop dough by a ¼-cup dry measure or a scoop about 4 inches apart onto an ungreased cookie sheet. Bake in a 350° oven about 15 minutes or until edges are lightly browned.

(Or, for small cookies, drop dough by a rounded teaspoon about 2 inches apart onto an ungreased cookie sheet. Bake in a 350° oven about 10 minutes.)

Cool for 1 minute on the cookie sheet. Transfer the cookies to a wire rack; cool. Makes about 26 large or about 60 small cookies.

Nutrition information per large cookie: *272 calories, 7 g protein, 32 g carbohydrate, 14 g fat (4 g saturated), 34 mg cholesterol, 173 mg sodium.*

White-Chocolate-Raspberry Cookies

If it's your turn to host the block party or the Christmas party, try these handsome melt-in-your-mouth cookies. They're elegant and sophisticated enough to serve as a simple dessert.

8 ounces white baking bars
½ cup butter
1 cup sugar
1 teaspoon baking soda
¼ teaspoon salt
2 eggs
2¾ cups all-purpose flour
½ cup seedless raspberry jam
3 ounces white baking bars
½ teaspoon shortening

Grease a cookie sheet. Set aside. Chop 4 ounces of the white baking bars. Set aside. In a heavy small saucepan heat another 4 ounces of the white baking bars over low heat until melted, stirring constantly. Cool.

In a large mixing bowl beat butter with an electric mixer on medium to high speed for 30 seconds. Add the sugar, baking soda, and salt; beat until combined. Beat in the eggs and melted white baking bars until combined. Beat in as much of the flour as you can with the mixer. Stir in any remaining flour with a wooden spoon. Stir in the 4 ounces chopped white baking bars.

Drop dough by a rounded teaspoon about 2 inches apart onto the prepared cookie sheet. Bake in a 375° oven for 7 to 9 minutes or until edges are lightly browned. Cool on cookie sheet for 1 minute. Transfer the cookies to a wire rack; cool.

Just before serving, in a small saucepan heat the raspberry jam over low heat until melted, stirring occasionally. Spoon about ½ teaspoon jam onto the top of each cookie.

In a heavy small saucepan combine the 3 ounces white baking bars and shortening. Heat over low heat until melted, stirring constantly. Drizzle over cookies. If necessary, chill about 15 minutes to firm baking bar mixture. Makes about 48 cookies.

Nutrition information per cookie: 104 calories, 1 g protein, 16 g carbohydrate, 4 g fat (2 g saturated), 14 mg cholesterol, 66 mg sodium.

Ultimate Bar Cookies

Crush any leftover bars and sprinkle over ice cream as a topping. (Pictured on page 231.)

2   cups all-purpose flour
½   cup packed brown sugar
½   cup butter, softened
1   cup coarsely chopped walnuts
1   3½-ounce jar macadamia nuts,
      coarsely chopped (1 cup)
1   6-ounce package white baking bars,
      coarsely chopped (1 cup)
1   cup milk chocolate pieces
¾   cup butter
½   cup packed brown sugar

In a medium bowl beat flour, ½ cup brown sugar, and ½ cup butter with an electric mixer on medium speed until mixture forms fine crumbs. Press into the bottom of an ungreased 13x9x2-inch baking pan. Bake in a 350° oven about 15 minutes or until lightly browned.

Transfer pan to a wire rack. Sprinkle nuts, baking bars, and milk chocolate pieces over hot crust. Cook and stir ¾ cup butter and ½ cup brown sugar until bubbly. Cook and stir for 1 minute more. Pour over nuts and chocolate in pan. Bake about 15 minutes more or just until bubbly around edges. Cool in pan on a wire rack. Cut into desired shapes. Makes 36 bars.

Nutrition information per bar: 188 calories, 2 g protein, 16 g carbohydrate, 13 g fat (6 g saturated), 18 mg cholesterol, 12 mg sodium.

Mocha Brownies

These buttery mocha brownies boast plenty of semisweet chocolate and a delightful hint of tangerine.

⅔   cup butter
⅓   cup unsweetened cocoa powder
1   teaspoon instant coffee crystals
1   cup granulated sugar
2   eggs
1   teaspoon vanilla
¾   cup all-purpose flour
½   cup semisweet chocolate pieces or
      chopped semisweet chocolate
1   teaspoon finely shredded tangerine
      or orange peel
      Powdered sugar (optional)

Grease an 8x8x2-inch baking pan. Set aside. In a medium saucepan melt butter. Stir in cocoa powder and coffee crystals. Remove from heat. Stir in the granulated sugar. Stir in eggs, one at a time, and vanilla. Beat lightly by hand just until combined. Stir in flour. Stir in chocolate pieces and shredded peel.

Spread into prepared pan. Bake in a 350° oven for 30 minutes. Cool in pan on a wire rack. If desired, sift powdered sugar over top. Cut into bars. Makes 24 brownies.

Nutrition information per brownie: 123 calories, 1 g protein, 13 g carbohydrate, 7 g fat (2 g saturated), 24 mg cholesterol, 52 mg sodium.

Citrus-Hazelnut Bars

Definitely a bar cookie with lots of appeal—these double citrus and nutty delights are not overly sweet and make a great accompaniment to an afternoon tea break.

⅓ cup butter
¼ cup granulated sugar
1 cup all-purpose flour
⅓ cup finely chopped hazelnuts (filberts) or chopped almonds, toasted
2 eggs
¾ cup granulated sugar
2 tablespoons all-purpose flour
1 teaspoon finely shredded orange peel
2 tablespoons orange juice
1 teaspoon finely shredded lemon peel
1 tablespoon lemon juice
½ teaspoon baking powder
Powdered sugar (optional)

For crust, in a medium mixing bowl beat the butter with an electric mixer on medium to high speed for 30 seconds. Add the ¼ cup granulated sugar. Beat until thoroughly combined. Beat in the 1 cup flour and about half of the nuts until mixture is crumbly.

Press mixture onto bottom of an ungreased 8x8x2-inch baking pan. Bake in a 350° oven about 10 minutes or until lightly browned.

Meanwhile, in a medium mixing bowl combine eggs, the ¾ cup granulated sugar, the 2 tablespoons flour, orange peel, orange juice, lemon peel, lemon juice, and baking powder. Beat on medium speed about 2 minutes or until combined. Pour over hot crust. Sprinkle with the remaining nuts.

Bake about 20 minutes more or until light brown around the edges and center is set. Cool in pan on a wire rack. If desired, sift powdered sugar over top. Cut into bars. Store bars, covered, in the refrigerator. Makes 20 bars.

Nutrition information per bar: 111 calories, 2 g protein, 16 g carbohydrate, 5 g fat (1 g saturated), 25 mg cholesterol, 43 mg sodium.

Creamy, Fudgy, Nutty Brownies

The creamy crown on these brownies is essentially a chocolate cheesecake mixture, so store them in the refrigerator.

---

4   ounces unsweetened chocolate,
     chopped
½   cup butter
1   cup all-purpose flour
½   cup chopped walnuts or pecans,
     toasted
¼   teaspoon baking powder
1½   cups sugar
3   eggs
1   teaspoon vanilla
3   ounces semisweet chocolate,
     chopped
2   3-ounce packages cream cheese,
     softened
¼   cup sugar
1   egg
1   tablespoon milk
½   teaspoon vanilla

Grease and lightly flour an 8x8x2-inch baking pan. Set aside. In a small saucepan heat the unsweetened chocolate and butter until melted, stirring occasionally. Remove from heat. Cool slightly. In a medium bowl stir together flour, nuts, and baking powder. Set aside.

In a large mixing bowl stir together melted chocolate mixture and 1½ cups sugar. Add the 3 eggs and the 1 teaspoon vanilla. Using a wooden spoon, lightly beat mixture just until combined (don't overbeat or brownies will rise too high, then fall). Stir in flour mixture.

Spread the brownie batter in the prepared pan. Bake in a 350° oven for 40 minutes.

Meanwhile, for topping, in a heavy small saucepan heat the semisweet chocolate over low heat until melted, stirring constantly. Cool slightly. In a medium mixing bowl beat the melted semisweet chocolate, softened cream cheese, the ¼ cup sugar, 1 egg, milk, and ½ teaspoon vanilla until combined.

Carefully spread topping evenly over hot brownies. Bake about 10 minutes more or until topping appears set. Cool in pan on a wire rack. Cover and chill at least 2 hours before serving. Cut into bars. Store bars, covered, in the refrigerator. Makes 12 brownies.

Nutrition information per brownie: 409 calories, 7 g protein, 43 g carbohydrate, 27 g fat (9 g saturated), 97 mg cholesterol, 143 mg sodium.

Ultimate Bar Cookies (recipe, page 228) and Creamy, Fudgy, Nutty Brownies

Sesame Pecan Wafers

Serve these nutty Southern-style wafers as a complement to a generous scoop of your favorite ice cream or frozen yogurt.

1	cup butter
⅔	cup sugar
1	teaspoon vanilla
1¾	cups all-purpose flour
½	cup sesame seed
½	cup ground pecans or almonds
2	ounces semisweet chocolate
½	teaspoon shortening

In a large mixing bowl beat butter with an electric mixer on medium to high speed for 30 seconds. Add the sugar and vanilla; beat until combined.

Beat in as much of the flour as you can with the mixer. Stir in the remaining flour, the sesame seed, and ground pecans or almonds.

Divide dough in half. If dough is too sticky to handle, wrap each half in waxed paper or plastic wrap and chill about 1 hour or until easy to handle.

On a lightly floured surface, roll each half of the dough to ⅛-inch thickness. Using 2-inch cookie cutters, cut dough into desired shapes. Place cookies about 1 inch apart on an ungreased cookie sheet.

Bake in a 375° oven for 7 to 8 minutes or until edges are lightly browned. Transfer cookies to a wire rack; cool.

In a heavy small saucepan combine the semisweet chocolate and shortening. Heat over low heat until melted, stirring occasionally. Drizzle chocolate mixture over cookies. Let cookies stand until chocolate is set. Makes about 56 cookies.

Nutrition information per cookie: 70 calories, 1 g protein, 6 g carbohydrate, 5 g fat (2 g saturated), 9 mg cholesterol, 34 mg sodium.

Swirled Mint Cookies

Dress up this spectacular sugar cookie for the holiday season by dipping the pressing glass into colored sugar crystals instead of granulated sugar.

1 cup butter
1 cup sugar
½ teaspoon baking powder
1 egg
1 teaspoon vanilla
½ teaspoon peppermint extract
2 cups all-purpose flour
10 drops red food coloring
10 drops green food coloring
Sugar

In a large mixing bowl beat butter with an electric mixer on medium to high speed for 30 seconds. Add 1 cup sugar and baking powder. Beat until fluffy. Beat in egg, vanilla, and peppermint extract. Beat in as much of the flour as you can with the mixer. Stir in the remaining flour with a wooden spoon.

Divide dough into 3 equal portions. Stir red food coloring into one portion, stir green food coloring into a second portion, and leave the third portion plain. Cover each portion with foil or plastic wrap and chill about 1 hour or till easy to handle.

Divide each color of dough into 4 equal portions. On a lightly floured surface, roll each portion into a ½-inch-diameter rope. Place a red, a green, and a plain rope side by side. Twist together. Repeat with the remaining ropes. Chill twisted ropes for 30 minutes.

Cut the ropes into ½-inch slices for larger cookies or ¼-inch slices for smaller ones. Carefully roll into balls, blending colors as little as possible. Place balls about 2 inches apart on an ungreased cookie sheet. Using a glass dipped in additional sugar, flatten each ball of dough to ¼-inch thickness.

Bake in a 375° oven for 8 to 10 minutes for larger cookies (6 to 8 minutes for smaller ones) or until edges are set. Transfer to a wire rack; cool. Makes about 72 large cookies or about 144 small cookies.

Nutrition information per large cookie: 46 calories, 0 g protein, 5 g carbohydrate, 3 g fat (2 g saturated), 10 mg cholesterol, 29 mg sodium.

Cranberry-Pecan Tassies

Fruit- and nut-filled tassies—old Scottish for "little cups"—dress up the after-dinner plate with their special-occasion flavor and homestyle comfort.

½ cup butter, softened
1 3-ounce package cream cheese, softened
1 cup all-purpose flour
1 egg
¾ cup packed brown sugar
1 teaspoon vanilla
Dash salt
⅓ cup finely chopped cranberries
3 tablespoons chopped pecans

For pastry, in a medium mixing bowl beat the butter and cream cheese with an electric mixer on medium to high speed until combined. Stir in the flour. If desired, chill the pastry for 1 hour.

Shape the pastry into 24 balls. Place pastry in ungreased 1¾-inch muffin cups. Press pastry evenly against the bottom and up the side of each muffin cup.

For filling, in another medium mixing bowl beat together the egg, brown sugar, vanilla, and salt just until smooth. Stir in the cranberries and pecans. Spoon the filling into the pastry-lined muffin cups.

Bake in a 325° oven for 30 to 35 minutes or until pastry is golden brown. Cool in muffin cups on wire racks. Remove tassies from muffin cups by running a knife around the edges. Makes 24 tassies.

Nutrition information per tassie: 94 calories, 1 g protein, 10 g carbohydrate, 6 g fat (3 g saturated), 23 mg cholesterol, 59 mg sodium.

STORING BAKED COOKIES

To store cookies after baking, cool completely; do not frost. In an airtight or freezer container, arrange cookies in a single layer; cover with a sheet of waxed paper. Repeat layers, leaving enough air space to close the container easily. Store at room temperature up to 3 days or freeze up to 8 months.

Jam Thumbprints

Have these cookies baked, cooled, and on hand for drop-in company. Fill them right before serving.

⅔ cup butter
½ cup sugar
2 egg yolks
1 teaspoon vanilla
1½ cups all-purpose flour
2 slightly beaten egg whites
1 cup finely chopped walnuts
⅓ to ½ cup apricot, strawberry, or
    cherry jam or preserves

Grease a cookie sheet. Set aside. In a large mixing bowl beat butter with an electric mixer on medium to high speed for 30 seconds. Add sugar; beat until combined, scraping side of bowl occasionally.

Beat in egg yolks and vanilla until combined. Beat in as much of the flour as you can with the mixer. Stir in the remaining flour. Cover and chill about 1 hour or until easy to handle.

Shape dough into 1-inch balls. Roll balls in egg whites, then coat with walnuts. Place about 1 inch apart on the prepared cookie sheet. Press your thumb into the center of each ball.

Bake in a 375° oven for 10 to 12 minutes or until edges are lightly browned. Transfer to a wire rack; cool. Before serving, fill centers of cookies with jam or preserves. Makes about 42 cookies.

Nutrition information per cookie: 79 calories, 1 g protein, 8 g carbohydrate, 5 g fat (2 g saturated), 18 mg cholesterol, 33 mg sodium.

ℳARGARINE IN BAKING

The recipes in this chapter call for butter, not margarine, because it ensures the best results. Although baked goods made with some margarines can be satisfactory, choosing the right margarine is tricky. Many margarines contain more water than oil, which will yield undesirable results. If you choose to use margarine, select a stick margarine that lists at least 80 percent vegetable oil or 100 calories per tablespoon on the package. Diet, whipped, liquid, and soft spreads or margarines are for table use—not baking. Their high water content can make baked goods wet and tough.

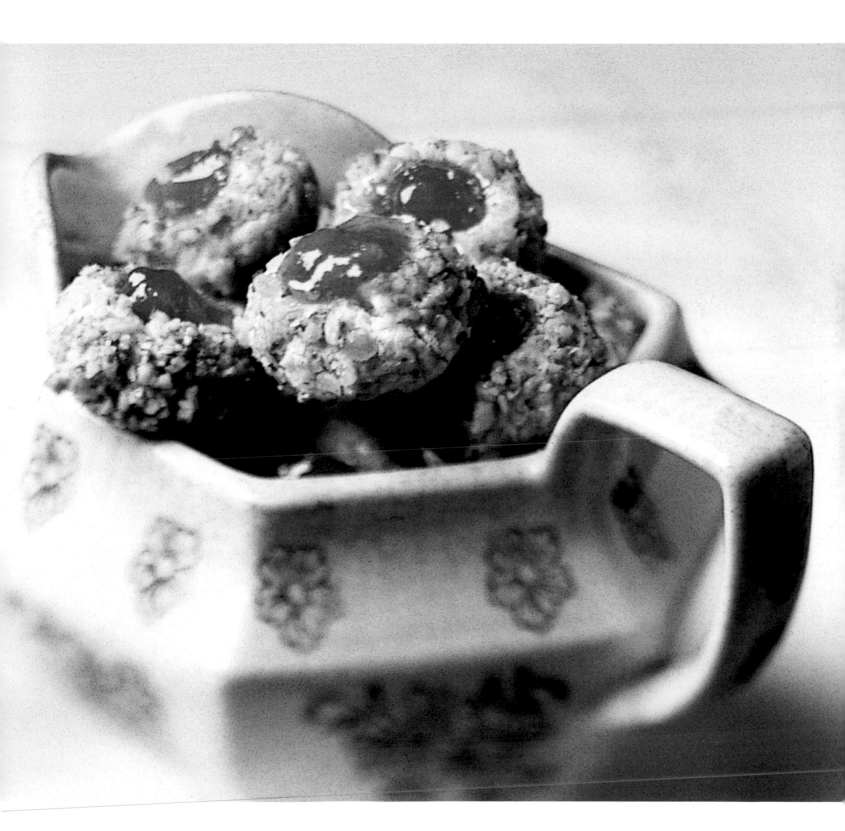

Oatmeal Cake

The natural goodness of rolled oats together with brown sugar and cinnamon give this old-fashioned cake its wonderful flavor.

1¼ cups boiling water
1 cup rolled oats
2 cups all-purpose flour
2 teaspoons baking powder
¾ teaspoon ground cinnamon
½ teaspoon baking soda
½ teaspoon salt
¼ teaspoon ground nutmeg
½ cup butter, softened
¾ cup granulated sugar
½ cup packed brown sugar
1 teaspoon vanilla
2 eggs
Broiled Nut Topping

Grease and lightly flour a 9-inch springform pan. Set aside. Pour boiling water over oats; stir until combined. Let stand for 20 minutes. In a medium bowl combine the flour, baking powder, cinnamon, baking soda, salt, and nutmeg. Set aside.

In a large mixing bowl beat butter with an electric mixer on medium to high speed for 30 seconds. Add granulated sugar, brown sugar, and vanilla; beat until combined. Add eggs, one at a time, beating well after each. Alternately add flour mixture and oat mixture, beating on low to medium speed after each addition just until combined. Pour the batter into prepared pan.

Bake in a 350° oven for 40 to 45 minutes or until a wooden toothpick inserted near the center comes out clean. Cool in pan on a wire rack for 20 minutes. Remove side of pan; cool cake on rack at least 1 hour.

Transfer cake to a baking sheet. Spread Broiled Nut Topping over cake. Broil about 4 inches from the heat for 2 to 3 minutes or until topping is bubbly and golden brown. Cool on wire rack before serving. Makes 12 servings.

Broiled Nut Topping: In a saucepan combine ¼ cup *butter* and 2 tablespoons *half-and-half, light cream,* or *milk*. Cook and stir over medium heat until butter is melted. Add ½ cup packed *brown sugar;* stir until sugar is dissolved. Remove from heat. Stir in ¾ cup chopped *pecans* or *walnuts* and ⅓ cup flaked *coconut*.

Nutrition information per serving: 388 calories, 5 g protein, 52 g carbohydrate, 18 g fat (9 g saturated), 67 mg cholesterol, 296 mg sodium.

Upside-Down Pineapple-Orange Cake

For a twist on pineapple upside-down cake, we added mandarin oranges, using half a can of pineapple slices and half a can of orange sections. If you prefer to make the cake with just one fruit, use a whole can.

⅔ cup packed brown sugar
6 tablespoons butter
1½ teaspoons finely shredded orange peel
1 11-ounce can mandarin orange sections
1 8-ounce can pineapple slices
1⅓ cups all-purpose flour
1¼ teaspoons baking powder
½ teaspoon salt
6 tablespoons butter
1 cup granulated sugar
¼ teaspoon almond extract
2 eggs
⅔ cup dairy sour cream
Sweetened Whipped Cream (optional)

In a saucepan combine brown sugar, 6 tablespoons butter, and orange peel. Cook and stir over medium heat until mixture is bubbly. Pour into an ungreased 9x9x2-inch baking pan.

Drain the oranges and pineapple. Cut half of the pineapple slices in half. Arrange the half slices of pineapple and half of the orange sections in pan. (Reserve remaining oranges and pineapple for another use.) Combine flour, baking powder, and salt.

In a large mixing bowl beat 6 tablespoons butter with an electric mixer on medium to high speed for 30 seconds. Add granulated sugar and almond extract; beat until combined. Add eggs, one at a time, beating well after each. Alternately add flour mixture and sour cream, beating on low to medium speed after each addition just until combined. Spoon over fruit.

Bake in a 350° oven for 35 to 40 minutes or until a wooden toothpick inserted near the center comes out clean. Cool in pan on a wire rack for 5 minutes. Invert onto a serving plate. Serve warm. If desired, top with Sweetened Whipped Cream. Makes 8 servings.

Sweetened Whipped Cream: In a chilled medium mixing bowl combine 1 cup *whipping cream*, 2 tablespoons *granulated sugar*, and ½ teaspoon *vanilla*. Beat with an electric mixer on medium to high speed until soft peaks form (tips curl).

Nutrition information per serving: 455 calories, 4 g protein, 64 g carbohydrate, 21 g fat (12 g saturated), 107 mg cholesterol, 371 mg sodium.

Banana Cake with Penuche Frosting

For a combination that's hard to beat, frost this easy-to-make cake right in the pan with the creamy brown sugar frosting.

2½ cups all-purpose flour
1½ cups granulated sugar
1½ teaspoons baking powder
1 teaspoon baking soda
½ teaspoon salt
1 cup mashed ripe bananas (about 3 bananas)
⅔ cup buttermilk or sour milk*
½ cup shortening
1 teaspoon vanilla
2 eggs
Penuche Frosting
Chopped nuts (optional)

Grease a 13x9x2-inch baking pan. Set aside. In a large mixing bowl combine flour, 1½ cups sugar, baking powder, baking soda, and salt. Add the bananas, buttermilk or sour milk, shortening, and vanilla.

Beat with an electric mixer on low speed until combined. Add eggs. Beat on medium speed for 2 minutes. Pour into the prepared pan.

Bake in a 350° oven about 35 minutes or until a wooden toothpick inserted near the center comes out clean. Cool completely in pan on a wire rack.

Frost with Penuche Frosting. If desired, immediately sprinkle with chopped nuts. Makes 12 to 16 servings.

*Note: To make ⅔ cup sour milk, place 2 teaspoons *lemon juice* or *vinegar* in a glass measuring cup. Add enough *milk* to make ⅔ cup total liquid; stir. Let stand for 5 minutes before using.

Penuche Frosting: In a medium saucepan melt ⅓ cup *butter* over medium heat. Stir in ⅔ cup packed *brown sugar.* Cook and stir until bubbly. Remove from heat. Add 3 tablespoons *milk,* beating vigorously until smooth. By hand, beat in enough sifted *powdered sugar* (about 2½ cups) to make a frosting of spreading consistency. Frost cake immediately.

Nutrition information per serving: 470 calories, 4 g protein, 82 g carbohydrate, 15 g fat (6 g saturated), 50 mg cholesterol, 274 mg sodium.

Busy-Day Cake

No time to bake? Stir up this one-bowl cake in only minutes with easy-to-keep-on-hand ingredients. Another time, skip the topping and serve it with fresh fruit and whipped cream.

1⅓ cups all-purpose flour
⅔   cup granulated sugar
2   teaspoons baking powder
⅔   cup milk
¼   cup butter, softened
1   egg
1   teaspoon vanilla
    Broiled Coconut Topping

Grease and flour an 8x1½-inch round baking pan. Set aside. In a large mixing bowl combine the flour, ⅔ cup sugar, and baking powder. Add the milk, butter, egg, and vanilla.

Beat with an electric mixer on low speed for 30 seconds. Beat on medium speed for 1 minute. Pour the batter into the prepared pan.

Bake in a 350° oven for 25 to 30 minutes or until a wooden toothpick inserted near the center comes out clean. Remove from heat.

Spread the Broiled Coconut Topping over the warm cake. Broil about 4 inches from the heat for 3 to 4 minutes or until topping is golden brown. Cool cake slightly in pan on a wire rack. Serve warm. Makes 8 servings.

Broiled Coconut Topping: In a medium mixing bowl stir together ¼ cup packed *brown sugar* and 2 tablespoons softened *butter*. Stir in 1 tablespoon *milk*. Stir in ½ cup flaked *coconut*, and, if desired, ¼ cup chopped *nuts*.

Nutrition information per serving: 281 calories, 4 g protein, 42 g carbohydrate, 11 g fat (6 g saturated), 51 mg cholesterol, 128 mg sodium.

Apple Cake

Generously rippled with apple slices and cinnamon and drizzled with powdered sugar icing, this luscious cake is especially welcome for breakfast or brunch on crisp autumn mornings.

¼ cup granulated sugar
2 tablespoons all-purpose flour
1½ teaspoons ground cinnamon
5 cups sliced, peeled cooking apples
2½ cups all-purpose flour
1½ cups granulated sugar
1½ teaspoons baking powder
½ teaspoon baking soda
1 cup cooking oil
4 eggs
¼ cup orange juice
2 teaspoons vanilla
   Powdered Sugar Icing

Grease and lightly flour a 10-inch fluted tube pan. Set aside. In a large mixing bowl combine ¼ cup sugar, 2 tablespoons flour, and cinnamon. Add apples; toss gently to coat. Set aside.

In another large mixing bowl combine 2½ cups flour, 1½ cups sugar, baking powder, and baking soda. Add oil, eggs, orange juice, and vanilla. Beat with an electric mixer on low to medium speed for 30 seconds. Beat on medium speed for 2 minutes.

Pour one-third of the batter (about 1½ cups) into the prepared pan. Top with half of the apple mixture. Spoon another one-third of the batter over apples in pan; top with the remaining apple mixture. Spoon the remaining batter over apples.

Bake in a 350° oven about 1¼ hours or until a wooden toothpick inserted near the center comes out clean.

Cool in pan on a wire rack for 15 minutes. Remove from pan. Cool completely on wire rack. Drizzle with Powdered Sugar Icing. Let cake stand for 1 to 2 hours before slicing. Makes 16 servings.

Powdered Sugar Icing: In a small mixing bowl combine 1 cup sifted *powdered sugar* and ¼ teaspoon *vanilla*. Stir in enough *milk* (2 to 4 teaspoons) to make an icing of drizzling consistency.

Nutrition information per serving: 338 calories, 4 g protein, 48 g carbohydrate, 15 g fat (2 g saturated), 53 mg cholesterol, 56 mg sodium.

Banana Split Cake

Looking for a star dessert for your next gathering? This one wins rave reviews for its soda fountain flavors.

1 package 2-layer-size banana cake mix
Sweetened Whipped Cream or 6 ounces frozen whipped dessert topping, thawed
1 cup sliced strawberries
1 8¼-ounce can crushed pineapple, well drained
1 11- to 12-ounce jar fudge ice-cream topping
½ cup coarsely chopped peanuts
Banana slices (optional)

Prepare the banana cake mix according to package directions for a two-layer cake. Cool completely.

For fillings, divide the Sweetened Whipped Cream or dessert topping in half. Fold strawberries into half of the whipped cream. Fold drained pineapple into the remaining whipped cream. In a small saucepan heat and stir fudge topping over low heat just until warm (not hot).

To assemble, using a serrated knife, split each cake layer in half horizontally. Place bottom of 1 split layer on serving plate. Top with the strawberry filling, spreading to edge of layer. Top with another split layer. Spread with half of the fudge topping, letting some drizzle down side. Sprinkle with half of the nuts.

Top with another split layer. Spread with pineapple filling. Top with remaining split layer. Spread with remaining fudge topping, letting some drizzle down side of cake. Sprinkle with the remaining nuts.

Serve the cake immediately. (Or, cover loosely with plastic wrap, placing a few toothpicks in top of cake so wrap doesn't stick to topping, and chill up to 2 hours.) If desired, garnish the cake with banana slices. Makes 12 servings.

Sweetened Whipped Cream: In a chilled medium mixing bowl combine 1 cup *whipping cream,* 2 tablespoons *sugar,* and ½ teaspoon *vanilla.* Beat with an electric mixer on medium to high speed until soft peaks form (tips curl).

Nutrition information per serving: 494 calories, 7 g protein, 67 g carbohydrate, 24 g fat (10 g saturated), 63 mg cholesterol, 222 mg sodium.

Chocolate Cream Cake

This trio of devil's food layers is first filled with vanilla butter cream, and then the entire cake is swirled with chocolaty cream cheese frosting—an irresistible combination!

2⅔   cups all-purpose flour
1½   teaspoons baking soda
¾   teaspoon salt
¾   cup butter
2¼   cups granulated sugar
2   teaspoons vanilla
3   eggs
3   ounces unsweetened chocolate,
     melted and cooled
1½   cups ice water
     Butter Cream Filling
     Chocolate-Cream Cheese Frosting

Grease and lightly flour three 9x1½- or 8x1½-inch round baking pans. Combine flour, baking soda, and salt.

In a large mixing bowl beat the butter with an electric mixer on medium to high speed for 30 seconds. Add 2¼ cups sugar and vanilla; beat until combined. Add eggs, one at a time, beating well after each. Beat in melted chocolate. Alternately add flour mixture and water, beating on low to medium speed after each addition just until combined. Pour batter into prepared pans.

Bake in a 350° oven for 25 to 30 minutes or until a wooden toothpick inserted near the centers comes out clean. Cool in pans on wire racks for 10 minutes. Remove from pans. Cool completely on wire racks.

Spread Butter Cream Filling on two of the layers; stack layers. Top with remaining layer. Frost cake with Chocolate-Cream Cheese Frosting. Store, covered, in the refrigerator. Makes 12 servings.

Butter Cream Filling: Beat ½ cup *butter* until softened. Beat in 2¼ cups sifted *powdered sugar*, 2 tablespoons *milk*, and ½ teaspoon *vanilla*. Beat in additional *milk*, if necessary, to make a filling of spreading consistency.

Chocolate-Cream Cheese Frosting: Beat ½ of an 8-ounce package *cream cheese* until softened. Beat in 3 tablespoons *milk*. Beat in 3¾ cups sifted *powdered sugar*. Beat in 3 ounces *unsweetened chocolate*, melted and cooled, and 1 teaspoon *vanilla*. Beat in additional *milk*, if necessary, to make a frosting of spreading consistency.

Nutrition information per serving: 730 calories, 7 g protein, 113 g carbohydrate, 32 g fat (17 g saturated), 115 mg cholesterol, 564 mg sodium.

Cream Cheese-Poppy Seed Pound Cake

Cream cheese and butter team up to ensure a moist texture and rich flavor in this melt-in-your-mouth cake.

1 cup butter
1 8-ounce package cream cheese
6 eggs
3 cups all-purpose flour
1 teaspoon baking powder
¼ teaspoon salt
2¼ cups granulated sugar
¼ cup poppy seed
2 teaspoons vanilla
  Lemon Icing

Bring the butter, cream cheese, and eggs to room temperature. Meanwhile, grease and lightly flour a 10-inch tube pan; set aside.

Combine flour, baking powder, and salt. Set aside. In a large mixing bowl beat butter and cream cheese with an electric mixer on medium to high speed about 30 seconds or until softened. Gradually add granulated sugar, 2 tablespoons at a time, beating on medium speed about 5 minutes or until very light and fluffy.

Add poppy seed and vanilla. Add eggs, one at a time, beating on low to medium speed for 1 minute after each addition and scraping bowl frequently. Gradually add flour mixture, beating on low speed just until combined. Pour batter into prepared pan.

Bake in a 325° oven about 1¼ hours or until a wooden toothpick inserted near center comes out clean. Cool in pan on a wire rack for 15 minutes. Remove from pan. Cool completely on wire rack. Drizzle with Lemon Icing. Makes 16 to 20 servings.

Lemon Icing: In a small bowl combine 1½ cups sifted *powdered sugar* and ½ teaspoon finely shredded *lemon peel*. Stir in enough *lemon juice* (1 to 2 tablespoons) to make an icing of drizzling consistency.

Nutrition information per serving: 415 calories, 6 g protein, 55 g carbohydrate, 19 g fat (11 g saturated), 126 mg cholesterol, 239 mg sodium.

Desserts

Contents

CHEESECAKE SUPREME
(recipe, page 263)

Peach Cobbler with Cinnamon-Swirl Biscuits

Many cobbler recipes have a drop biscuit topping, but this one has tender biscuit slices filled with a nut-and-spice mixture.

1	cup all-purpose flour
1	tablespoon brown sugar
1½	teaspoons baking powder
¼	teaspoon salt
⅛	teaspoon baking soda
¼	cup butter
⅓	cup milk
½	cup finely chopped walnuts
3	tablespoons brown sugar
¼	teaspoon ground cinnamon
1	tablespoon butter, melted
⅔	cup packed brown sugar
4	teaspoons cornstarch
½	teaspoon finely shredded lemon peel
6	cups sliced peeled peaches or 6 cups frozen unsweetened peach slices
⅔	cup water

For biscuits, in a medium mixing bowl stir together flour, 1 tablespoon brown sugar, baking powder, salt, and baking soda.

With a pastry blender, cut in ¼ cup butter until the mixture resembles coarse crumbs. Make a well in the center. Add milk all at once. Using a fork, stir just until dough forms a ball.

On a lightly floured surface, knead dough gently for 10 to 12 strokes. Roll or pat dough into a 12x6-inch rectangle. Combine walnuts, 3 tablespoons brown sugar, and cinnamon. Brush dough with melted butter and sprinkle with nut mixture. Starting from a short side, roll up jelly-roll style. Seal edge. Cut into six 1-inch slices. Set aside.

For filling, in a large saucepan stir together ⅔ cup brown sugar, cornstarch, and lemon peel. Add peaches and water. Cook and stir until thickened and bubbly.

Pour the hot filling into an ungreased 2-quart rectangular baking dish. Arrange the biscuit slices, cut sides down, on hot filling. Bake in a 375° oven about 25 minutes or until biscuits are golden brown. Makes 6 servings.

Nutrition information per serving: 436 calories, 5 g protein, 71 g carbohydrate, 17 g fat (3 g saturated), 13 mg cholesterol, 315 mg sodium.

Country Pear and Cherry Crisp

Country Pear and Cherry Crisp

The topping stays extra-crunchy, and the best part is that it's a simple combination of granola and butter.

1	16-ounce package frozen unsweetened pitted tart red cherries, thawed, or one 16-ounce can pitted tart red cherries (water pack)
⅓ to ½	cup sugar
2	tablespoons all-purpose flour
1	teaspoon finely shredded orange peel
½	teaspoon ground cinnamon
3 to 4	medium pears, peeled, cored, and thinly sliced (3 cups)
1½	cups granola
2	tablespoons butter, melted
	Vanilla ice cream (optional)

If using canned cherries, drain cherries, reserving ½ cup juice. In a large mixing bowl combine frozen or canned cherries and reserved juice. Add sugar and toss to coat. Let stand for 5 minutes.

Combine flour, orange peel, and cinnamon. Sprinkle over cherries; toss to mix. Add pears; toss to mix. Transfer to an ungreased 2-quart square baking dish. Combine granola and butter; sprinkle over filling.

Bake in a 375° oven about 30 minutes or until pears are tender. If necessary, cover with foil the last 5 to 10 minutes to prevent overbrowning. Serve warm. If desired, serve with ice cream. Makes 6 servings.

Nutrition information per serving: 318 calories, 4 g protein, 58 g carbohydrate, 10 g fat (4 g saturated), 5 mg cholesterol, 94 mg sodium.

Red Wine-Marinated Peaches

Embellish this golden fruit with red wine, cinnamon, and cloves.

6	ripe medium peaches, peeled, pitted, and sliced, or pears, cored and sliced
1½	cups fruity red wine (such as Beaujolais) or dry white wine
¾	cup sugar
½	teaspoon ground cinnamon
⅛	teaspoon ground cloves

Place peaches or pears in a large bowl. For marinade, in a medium saucepan combine the wine, sugar, cinnamon, and cloves. Cook and stir over medium heat until sugar is dissolved.

Pour the marinade over peaches; toss gently to coat. Marinate at room temperature for 30 to 60 minutes, stirring occasionally. To serve, spoon the peaches and the marinade into dessert dishes. Makes 6 servings.

Nutrition information per serving: 262 calories, 1 g protein, 51 g carbohydrate, 0 g fat (0 g saturated), 0 mg cholesterol, 6 mg sodium.

Gingered Shortcake with Spiced Fruit

Shortcake isn't just for summer berries anymore! Enjoy this warming dessert with fall fruits such as apples, persimmons, or pears. The shortcake can be made ahead and refrigerated, then warmed—wrapped in foil—in a 350° oven about 25 minutes.

Gingered Shortcake
1 cup whipping cream
2 tablespoons granulated sugar
½ teaspoon vanilla
3 tablespoons butter
3 medium cooking apples, Fuyu persimmons, and/or pears, cored (if necessary) and thinly sliced
3 tablespoons brown sugar
¼ teaspoon ground nutmeg
1 cup blueberries

Prepare Gingered Shortcake. In a chilled bowl combine cream, granulated sugar, and vanilla. Beat with chilled beaters of an electric mixer until soft peaks form. Cover and chill.

In a large skillet melt butter over medium heat. Add apples, persimmons, and/or pears. Cook for 2 to 5 minutes or until almost tender. Stir in brown sugar and nutmeg. Cook for 1 to 3 minutes more or until tender. Stir in blueberries.

Place bottom cake layer on serving plate. Spoon about two-thirds of the fruit mixture and half of the whipped cream over cake. Top with second cake layer and remaining fruit mixture. Pass remaining whipped cream. Makes 8 servings.

Gingered Shortcake: Combine 2 cups *all-purpose flour,* ¼ cup *granulated sugar,* and 2 teaspoons *baking powder.* Cut in ½ cup *butter* until mixture resembles coarse crumbs. Combine 1 beaten *egg,* ⅔ cup *milk,* and 1 tablespoon grated *gingerroot;* add to flour mixture. Stir just to moisten. Spread in a greased 8x1½-inch round baking pan. Bake in a 450° oven for 18 to 20 minutes or until a wooden toothpick inserted near the center comes out clean. Cool in pan for 10 minutes. Remove shortcake from pan; cool on a wire rack for 30 minutes. Split the shortcake into 2 layers.

Nutrition information per serving: 457 calories, 5 g protein, 47 g carbohydrate, 28 g fat (17 g saturated), 111 mg cholesterol, 280 mg sodium.

Gingered Melon

Enjoy this cool, refreshing melon cup on the hottest days of summer.

¾ cup water
½ cup sugar
2 teaspoons finely shredded lemon peel (set aside)
4 teaspoons lemon juice
1½ to 2 teaspoons grated gingerroot
4 cups watermelon, cantaloupe, and/or honeydew melon balls
⅓ cup flaked coconut

For syrup, in a small saucepan combine water, sugar, lemon juice, and gingerroot. Bring to boiling; reduce heat. Simmer, uncovered, for 3 minutes. Remove from heat; stir in lemon peel. Cool to room temperature. If desired, strain syrup. Pour over melon. Stir gently to coat. Cover and chill for 2 to 24 hours.

To serve, spoon melon and syrup into dessert dishes. Sprinkle with coconut. Makes 6 servings.

Nutrition information per serving: 122 calories, 1 g protein, 28 g carbohydrate, 2 g fat (1 g saturated), 0 mg cholesterol, 10 mg sodium.

Honey-Fruit Pizza

Pretty as a picture, this fresh-tasting masterpiece features a cookie crust, summer fruits, and a honey glaze.

¾ cup butter
⅓ cup sifted powdered sugar
2 cups all-purpose flour
2 tablespoons honey
1 tablespoon cornstarch
⅓ cup apple or orange juice
2 tablespoons currant or apple jelly
1 cup sliced strawberries
1 medium nectarine, pitted and sliced, or 1 medium peach, peeled, pitted, and sliced
½ cup blueberries or raspberries
½ cup seedless green or red grapes, halved

For crust, beat butter with an electric mixer on medium speed for 30 seconds. Beat in the powdered sugar. Gradually add flour, beating until well mixed. Pat into a greased 11- or 12-inch pizza pan. Bake in a 375° oven for 15 to 18 minutes or until crust is golden brown. Cool in pan on a wire rack.

For glaze, stir together honey and cornstarch. Stir in juice and jelly. Cook and stir until thickened and bubbly. Cook and stir for 2 minutes more. Remove from heat. Cool for 5 minutes (do not stir). Spread half of the glaze over crust. Top with fruit and the remaining glaze. Chill at least 30 minutes before serving. Makes 12 servings.

Nutrition information per serving: 223 calories, 2 g protein, 28 g carbohydrate, 12 g fat (7 g saturated), 31 mg cholesterol, 118 mg sodium.

Gingered Melon

Chocolate-Irish Cream Cheesecake

Impress your guests with this home-baked version of a favorite often found on dessert carts in fine restaurants.

1 cup finely crushed chocolate wafers (about 17 cookies)*
¼ cup butter or margarine, melted
½ teaspoon ground cinnamon
3 8-ounce packages cream cheese, softened
1 8-ounce carton dairy sour cream
1 8-ounce package semisweet chocolate, melted and cooled
1 cup sugar
3 eggs
½ cup Irish cream liqueur**
2 tablespoons whipping cream or milk
2 teaspoons vanilla
⅓ cup semisweet chocolate pieces, melted (optional)

For crust, in a small bowl combine crushed wafers, butter or margarine, and cinnamon. Press mixture onto the bottom of an ungreased 9- or 10-inch* springform pan. Set aside.

For filling, in a large bowl beat cream cheese, sour cream, the 8 ounces melted chocolate, and sugar with an electric mixer on medium to high speed until smooth. Add eggs all at once. Beat on low speed just until combined. Stir in liqueur, cream or milk, and vanilla.

Pour into prepared pan. Place springform pan in a shallow baking pan. Bake in a 325° oven for 50 to 60 minutes or until center appears nearly set when shaken.

Cool in springform pan on a wire rack for 15 minutes. Loosen the cheesecake from side of pan; cool for 30 minutes more. Remove side of pan; cool for 1 hour. Cover and chill for 4 to 24 hours. To serve, if desired, drizzle cheesecake with the ⅓ cup melted chocolate. Makes 12 to 16 servings.

*Note: If using a 10-inch springform pan, use 1¼ cups crushed chocolate wafers for the crust.

**Note: If you prefer to use less liqueur, substitute whipping cream or milk for some of the liqueur.

Nutrition information per serving: 525 calories, 7 g protein, 34 g carbohydrate, 37 g fat (20 g saturated), 134 mg cholesterol, 295 mg sodium.

Cheesecake Supreme

Check for doneness by gently shaking the pan rather than inserting a knife, which will make a crack. When the cheesecake is done, a 1-inch area in the center will jiggle a little: this area will firm after cooling.

1¾ cups finely crushed graham crackers
¼ cup finely chopped walnuts
½ teaspoon ground cinnamon
½ cup butter or margarine, melted
2 8-ounce packages cream cheese, softened
1 cup sugar
2 tablespoons all-purpose flour
1 teaspoon vanilla
½ teaspoon finely shredded lemon peel (optional)
2 eggs
1 egg yolk
¼ cup milk
Raspberries (optional)
Raspberry Sauce (optional)

For crust, combine the graham crackers, walnuts, and cinnamon. Stir in butter or margarine. If desired, reserve ¼ cup of the crumb mixture for topping. Press the remaining crumb mixture onto the bottom and about 2 inches up the side of an 8- or 9-inch springform pan.

For filling, in a large mixing bowl beat cream cheese, sugar, flour, vanilla, and, if desired, lemon peel with an electric mixer on low speed until combined. Add eggs and egg yolk all at once. Beat on low speed just until combined. Stir in milk. Pour into the prepared pan. If desired, sprinkle with the reserved crumbs.

Place springform pan in a shallow baking pan. Bake in a 375° oven for 45 to 50 minutes for the 8-inch pan (35 to 40 minutes for the 9-inch pan) or until center appears nearly set when shaken.

Cool in pan on a wire rack for 15 minutes. Loosen crust from pan. Cool for 30 minutes more. Remove side of pan. Cool completely. Cover and chill at least 4 hours. If desired, garnish with raspberries and serve with Raspberry Sauce. Makes 12 to 16 servings.

Raspberry Sauce: In a blender container cover and blend 3 cups fresh or thawed, frozen *raspberries* (do not drain), half at a time, until smooth. Press berries through a sieve; discard seeds. In a saucepan combine ⅓ cup *sugar* and 1 teaspoon *cornstarch*. Add sieved berries. Cook and stir until thickened and bubbly. Cook and stir for 2 minutes more. Cool. Makes about 1 cup.

Nutrition information per serving: 429 calories, 7 g protein, 30 g carbohydrate, 32 g fat (18 g saturated), 137 mg cholesterol, 329 mg sodium.

Apple-Blueberry Pastries

Take a platter of these petite pastries to your next potluck.

2   tablespoons sugar
1   tablespoon cornstarch
2   medium apples, peeled, cored,
      and chopped (about 2 cups)
½   cup fresh or frozen blueberries
1½ teaspoons water
½   teaspoon finely shredded
      orange peel
1   17¼-ounce package (2 sheets)
      frozen puff pastry
    Easy Orange Icing
    Edible flowers (optional)

Line a large baking sheet with foil; set aside. For filling, in a medium saucepan stir together the sugar and cornstarch. Add apples, blueberries, and water. Cook and stir over medium heat until thickened and bubbly. Cook and stir for 2 minutes more. Stir in orange peel. Remove from heat. Cool completely.

Let folded puff pastry thaw at room temperature for 20 minutes. On a lightly floured surface, unfold and roll each sheet of pastry into a 15x10-inch rectangle. Cut each sheet into ten 5x3-inch rectangles.

Spoon about 1 tablespoon of the filling on half of each rectangle to within ½ inch of edges. Brush edges with water. Starting from a short side, lift pastry up and over filling. Press edges with the tines of a fork to seal. Place on the prepared baking sheet.

Bake in a 375° oven for 18 to 20 minutes or until golden. Remove and cool on a wire rack. Drizzle with Easy Orange Icing. If desired, garnish with edible flowers. Makes 20 pastries.

Easy Orange Icing: In a small mixing bowl stir together 1 cup sifted *powdered sugar,* 1 tablespoon *orange juice,* and ¼ teaspoon *vanilla.* Stir in additional *orange juice,* 1 teaspoon at a time, to make an icing of drizzling consistency.

Nutrition information per pastry: 142 calories, 1 g protein, 18 g carbohydrate, 8 g fat (0 g saturated), 0 mg cholesterol, 92 mg sodium.

Fruit Tart with Amaretto Creme

Use your 9-inch springform pan for this luscious almond and fruit tart.

Pastry for Single-Crust Pie
Milk
1   tablespoon granulated sugar
1   8-ounce package cream cheese,
      softened
1   3-ounce package cream cheese,
      softened
½   cup amaretto
3   tablespoons brown sugar
½   cup finely chopped almonds, toasted
3   to 4 cups chilled assorted fresh fruit
1   tablespoon granulated sugar

Prepare Pastry for Single-Crust Pie. On a lightly floured surface, roll pastry into an 11-inch circle. Ease into a 9-inch springform pan. Press evenly onto the bottom and 1 inch up side of pan. If desired, flute edge. Generously prick bottom and side with tines of a fork. Line with a double thickness of foil.

Bake in a 450° oven for 5 minutes. Remove foil. Brush edge of pastry with milk. Sprinkle with 1 tablespoon granulated sugar. Bake for 7 to 9 minutes more or until pastry is golden brown. Cool completely in pan on a wire rack.

In a small bowl beat cream cheese, amaretto, and brown sugar with an electric mixer on medium speed until smooth. Stir in almonds. Spread over cooled pastry. Serve immediately or chill up to 4 hours.

To serve, top the cream cheese mixture with desired fruit. Remove side of pan. If desired, remove bottom of pan. Sprinkle the fruit with 1 tablespoon granulated sugar. Makes 8 servings.

Pastry for Single-Crust Pie: In a medium bowl stir together 1¼ cups *all-purpose flour* and ¼ teaspoon *salt*. Using a pastry blender, cut in ⅓ cup *shortening* until pieces are pea-size. Using 4 to 5 tablespoons *cold water*, sprinkle 1 tablespoon water at a time over mixture, gently tossing with a fork until all is moistened. Form dough into a ball.

Nutrition information per serving: 398 calories, 6 g protein, 35 g carbohydrate, 26 g fat (9 g saturated), 51 mg cholesterol, 226 mg sodium.

Cherry-Pear Pie

The surprise ingredient in this pie is a subtle hint of rosemary that enhances the fresh fruit flavors of the pears and red cherries.

⅔ cup granulated sugar
3 tablespoons cornstarch
¼ teaspoon ground nutmeg
¼ teaspoon dried rosemary, crushed
    (optional)
4 cups thinly sliced, peeled pears
3 cups frozen pitted tart red cherries
    Pastry for Double-Crust Pie
1 beaten egg white
1 tablespoon water
    Coarse sugar
    Vanilla ice cream (optional)

For filling, in a large mixing bowl stir together ⅔ cup sugar, cornstarch, nutmeg, and, if desired, rosemary. Add sliced pears and frozen red cherries. Toss gently to coat. Let mixture stand at room temperature for 20 minutes.

Meanwhile, prepare Pastry for Double-Crust Pie. On a lightly floured surface, roll out half of the pastry. Ease into a 9-inch pie plate.

Transfer the filling to the pastry-lined pie plate. Trim pastry even with edge of pie plate. Roll out remaining pastry. Using a miniature heart cookie cutter, cut out shapes from center of pastry. Set cutouts aside. Place the pastry on top of filling; trim to ½ inch beyond edge of pie plate. Fold the top pastry under bottom pastry. Seal and flute edge. Cover the edge with foil.

In a small bowl combine egg white and water. Brush pastry with some of the egg white mixture. Top with pastry cutouts. Brush again with egg white mixture. Sprinkle with coarse sugar.

Bake in a 375° oven for 25 minutes. Remove foil. Bake for 30 to 35 minutes more or until crust is golden brown. Cool slightly on wire rack. Serve warm. If desired, serve with ice cream. Makes 8 servings.

Pastry for Double-Crust Pie: In a large mixing bowl stir together 2 cups *all-purpose flour* and ½ teaspoon *salt*. Using a pastry blender, cut in ⅔ cup *shortening* until the pieces are pea-size. Using 6 to 7 tablespoons *cold water*, sprinkle 1 tablespoon water at a time over mixture, gently tossing with a fork until all is moistened. Divide in half. Form each half into a ball.

Nutrition information per serving: 418 calories, 4 g protein, 62 g carbohydrate, 18 g fat (4 g saturated), 0 mg cholesterol, 143 mg sodium.

No-Peel Apple Pie

The expression "easy-as-pie" surely applies to this home-style treat. Pick a thin-skinned apple, such as Golden Delicious, Jonagold, or Jonathan, to make it.

1	15-ounce package (2 crusts) folded refrigerated unbaked piecrust
6	large cooking apples
½	cup water
2	tablespoons lemon juice
½	cup granulated sugar
2	tablespoons all-purpose flour
1½	teaspoons apple pie spice
	Whipping cream or milk
	Coarse and/or granulated sugar

Let refrigerated piecrust stand at room temperature according to package directions. Unfold the piecrust. Ease one crust into a 9-inch pie plate. Set aside.

For filling, core and slice unpeeled apples (you should have 8 cups). In a large mixing bowl combine the apples, water, and lemon juice. Toss gently to coat. In another large mixing bowl stir together the ½ cup sugar, flour, and apple pie spice. Drain the apples well; add to sugar mixture. Toss gently to coat.

Transfer the filling to the pastry-lined pie plate. Trim pastry even with edge of pie plate. Cut out desired small shapes from center of the remaining piecrust. Set cutouts aside.

Place piecrust on top of filling; trim to ½ inch beyond edge of pie plate. Fold the top pastry under bottom pastry. Seal and flute edge. Cover edge with foil. Brush the pastry with a little whipping cream or milk. Top with pastry cutouts. Brush again with cream or milk. Sprinkle with coarse and/or granulated sugar.

Bake in a 375° oven for 30 minutes. Remove foil. Bake about 30 minutes more or until crust is golden brown. Cool slightly on a wire rack. Serve warm. Makes 8 servings.

Nutrition information per serving: 373 calories, 2 g protein, 58 g carbohydrate, 16 g fat (1 g saturated), 18 mg cholesterol, 211 mg sodium.

Pumpkin Pecan Pie

Filled with lots of crunchy pecans, this special dessert will become a must at your Thanksgiving celebration.

3 slightly beaten eggs
1 15-ounce can pumpkin
¾ cup sugar
½ cup dark-colored corn syrup
1 teaspoon vanilla
¾ teaspoon ground cinnamon
1 unbaked 9-inch piecrust
1 cup chopped pecans
   Whipped cream (optional)
   Ground cinnamon (optional)

In a medium mixing bowl combine eggs, pumpkin, sugar, corn syrup, vanilla, and ¾ teaspoon cinnamon; mix well. Pour into piecrust. Sprinkle with pecans.

Bake in a 350° oven for 50 to 55 minutes or until a knife inserted near center comes out clean. Cool on a wire rack. Refrigerate within 2 hours; cover for longer storage. If desired, serve pie with whipped cream and sprinkle with additional cinnamon. Makes 8 servings.

Nutrition information per serving: 412 calories, 6 g protein, 55 g carbohydrate, 20 g fat (4 g saturated), 80 mg cholesterol, 108 mg sodium.

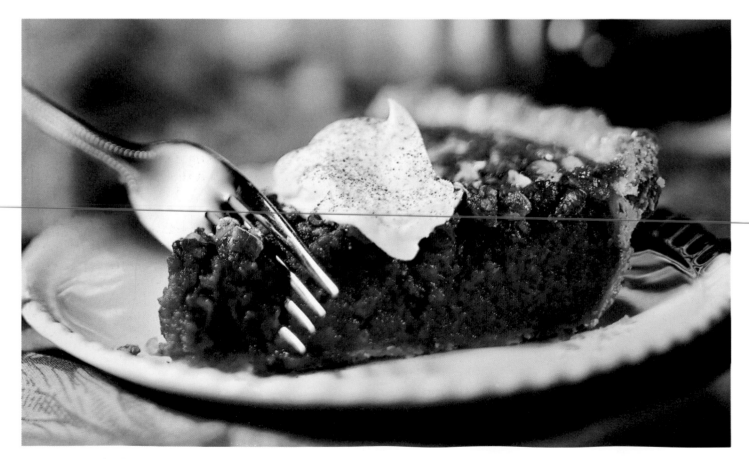

Rice Pudding

This creamy rice pudding is a soothing conclusion to a spicy meal.

½ cup golden raisins
¼ cup rum
3 cups milk
½ cup long grain rice
3 inches stick cinnamon
¼ cup sugar
1 teaspoon vanilla
   Ground cinnamon

In a small bowl combine raisins and rum. Set aside. In a heavy medium saucepan combine milk, uncooked rice, and stick cinnamon. Bring to boiling; reduce heat. Cover and simmer about 20 minutes or until rice is tender. Remove stick cinnamon.

Drain the raisins, discarding rum. Stir the raisins, sugar, and vanilla into rice mixture. Sprinkle with ground cinnamon. Serve warm or chilled. Makes 6 servings.

Nutrition information per serving: 200 calories, 6 g protein, 38 g carbohydrate, 3 g fat (2 g saturated), 9 mg cholesterol, 64 mg sodium.

Brownie Pudding

As this homey dessert bakes, a layer of cake magically rises to the top, leaving a chocolaty sauce underneath.

1 cup all-purpose flour
¾ cup granulated sugar
2 tablespoons unsweetened cocoa powder
2 teaspoons baking powder
¼ teaspoon salt
½ cup milk
2 tablespoons cooking oil
1 teaspoon vanilla
½ cup chopped walnuts
¾ cup packed brown sugar
¼ cup unsweetened cocoa powder
1½ cups boiling water

Grease an 8x8x2-inch baking pan; set aside. In a medium mixing bowl stir together the flour, granulated sugar, 2 tablespoons cocoa powder, baking powder, and salt. Stir in the milk, cooking oil, and vanilla. Stir in walnuts.

Pour into the prepared pan. In another medium bowl stir together brown sugar and ¼ cup cocoa powder. Stir in the boiling water; slowly pour over batter. Bake in a 350° oven for 40 minutes. Cool on a wire rack for 45 to 60 minutes. Serve warm. Makes 6 to 8 servings.

Nutrition information per serving: 368 calories, 5 g protein, 65 g carbohydrate, 12 g fat (2 g saturated), 2 mg cholesterol, 271 mg sodium.

Orange Bread Pudding with Warm Maple Sauce

So much flavor, so little fat—this bread pudding seemingly has it all.

4	slices white or whole wheat bread
⅓	cup raisins
3	eggs
2	egg whites
1¾	cups milk
⅓	cup orange marmalade
¼	cup sugar
½	teaspoon ground cinnamon
½	teaspoon vanilla
	Maple Sauce
	Orange slices, halved

Cut bread into 2-inch strips. Spread strips in a large shallow baking pan. Bake in a 325° oven for 10 to 15 minutes or until dry, stirring twice. Transfer strips to an ungreased 8x1½-inch round baking pan. Sprinkle with raisins. Set aside.

In a medium mixing bowl beat together eggs, egg whites, milk, orange marmalade, sugar, cinnamon, and vanilla with a wire whisk, fork, or rotary beater. Pour over bread and raisins in pan.

Bake in the 325° oven about 55 minutes or until a knife inserted near the center comes out clean. Cool slightly on a wire rack. Serve the bread pudding warm with warm Maple Sauce and garnish with orange slices. Makes 6 servings.

Maple Sauce: In a small saucepan combine 1 tablespoon *cornstarch* and ¼ teaspoon finely shredded *orange peel*. Stir in ¾ cup *orange juice* and ⅓ cup *maple-flavored syrup*. Cook and stir until thickened and bubbly. Cook and stir for 2 minutes more. Remove from heat. Stir in 1 teaspoon *butter* or *margarine*. Makes about 1 cup.

Nutrition information per serving: 299 calories, 9 g protein, 56 g carbohydrate, 5 g fat (2 g saturated), 113 mg cholesterol, 187 mg sodium.

Ginger Custard with Plum Sauce

For a rosy red sauce, choose a variety of plums with red skin, such as Red Beaut, Ace, or Queen Ann.

4 slightly beaten eggs
2 cups milk
½ cup sugar
1 teaspoon vanilla
½ teaspoon ground ginger
6 fresh medium plums, pitted and coarsely chopped (2½ cups)
⅓ cup sugar
1 tablespoon lemon juice
1 tablespoon water
1½ teaspoons cornstarch
½ teaspoon vanilla

In a medium mixing bowl combine eggs, milk, ½ cup sugar, 1 teaspoon vanilla, and ginger. Beat until well combined but not foamy. Place six 6-ounce custard cups in a large shallow baking pan on oven rack. Pour egg mixture into custard cups. Pour hot water into pan around custard cups to reach halfway up sides of cups.

Bake in a 350° oven for 30 to 35 minutes or until a knife inserted near centers comes out clean. Remove cups from water. Cool on a wire rack at least 20 minutes.

Meanwhile, for plum sauce, in a medium saucepan combine plums, ⅓ cup sugar, and lemon juice. Bring to boiling; reduce heat. Cover and simmer about 8 minutes or until plums are tender. Stir together water and cornstarch. Stir into plum mixture. Cook and stir until thickened and bubbly. Cook and stir for 2 minutes more. Remove from heat. Stir in ½ teaspoon vanilla.

To serve, unmold the custards onto dessert plates. Spoon the plum sauce over custards. Makes 6 servings.

Nutrition information per serving: 241 calories, 7 g protein, 42 g carbohydrate, 5 g fat (2 g saturated), 148 mg cholesterol, 83 mg sodium.

*P*ERFECTLY RIPE PLUMS

To purchase plums at their peak, look for firm, plump, well-shaped fruit with good color for its variety. Press a plum gently; it should give slightly. The bloom (light gray cast) on the skin is natural protection and doesn't affect quality. Avoid overly soft, bruised, or very hard fruit. To ripen plums at home, store at room temperature for 1 to 2 days. Then refrigerate them for up to 5 days.

Cinnamon Meringues with Fruit

For crispy meringue shells, serve them right away. However, if you like softer, marshmallowlike shells, chill them for up to 2 hours before serving.

2 egg whites
½ teaspoon ground cinnamon
½ teaspoon vanilla
¼ teaspoon cream of tartar
½ cup sugar
2 cups sliced peeled peaches or sliced nectarines
2 tablespoons sugar
1 tablespoon cornstarch
2 cups fresh fruit (such as sliced peeled peaches or kiwifruit and/or sliced nectarines or strawberries)

For meringue shells, cover a baking sheet with plain brown paper (specially made for baking). Draw six 3-inch squares or six 3½-inch circles on the paper. In a small mixing bowl beat the egg whites, cinnamon, vanilla, and cream of tartar with an electric mixer on medium speed until soft peaks form. Gradually add the ½ cup sugar, beating on high speed until stiff peaks form and sugar is almost dissolved.

Spoon meringue mixture into a decorating bag fitted with a medium plain-round or star tip (about ¼-inch opening). Pipe shells onto the prepared baking sheet. (Or, using a spoon or a spatula, spread the meringue mixture over the squares or circles on the prepared baking sheet, building up sides to form shells.)

Bake in a 300° oven for 30 minutes. Turn off the heat and let meringue shells dry in the oven with the door closed for at least 1 hour. (Do not open oven.) Peel off paper.

For sauce, place 2 cups peaches or nectarines in a blender container or food processor bowl. Cover and blend or process until nearly smooth. Pour into a saucepan. Mix 2 tablespoons sugar and cornstarch; stir into peach mixture. Cook and stir until thickened and bubbly. Cook and stir for 2 minutes more.

To serve, place meringue shells on dessert plates. Spoon the sauce into meringue shells. Top with fresh fruit. Serve immediately or cover and chill up to 2 hours. Makes 6 servings.

Nutrition information per serving: 138 calories, 2 g protein, 34 g carbohydrate, 0 g fat (0 g saturated), 0 mg cholesterol, 19 mg sodium.

Frosty Chocolate-Cherry Yogurt

Yogurt swirled with cherries and chocolate makes a cool, creamy, and scrumptious alternative to ice cream.

2 16-ounce cartons (3½ cups) vanilla
    yogurt (no gelatin added)*
2½ cups fresh or frozen pitted dark
    sweet cherries
⅓ cup milk
⅓ cup light-colored corn syrup
½ cup miniature semisweet
    chocolate pieces
    Fresh dark sweet cherries (optional)

In a blender container or food processor bowl combine yogurt, 1 cup of the pitted cherries, milk, and corn syrup. Cover and blend or process until mixture is almost smooth. (If using a food processor, process half at a time.)

Freeze in a 2-quart ice-cream freezer according to manufacturer's directions until almost firm. Add the remaining pitted cherries and chocolate. Continue to freeze as directed until firm. If desired, serve with additional fresh cherries. Makes 12 servings.

*Note: Yogurt without gelatin gives this dessert a better texture. Check the ingredients on the label.

Nutrition information per serving: 299 calories, 8 g protein, 55 g carbohydrate, 8 g fat (2 g saturated), 9 mg cholesterol, 107 mg sodium.

English Toffee Ice Cream

If you're making this frozen treat for kids, substitute milk for the coffee.

4 1.4-ounce bars chocolate-covered
    English toffee
2 cups whipping cream
1 14-ounce can sweetened
    condensed milk
½ cup strong coffee, cooled
1½ teaspoons vanilla

Crush toffee bars by placing them between two pieces of waxed paper and crushing them with a rolling pin. Set aside. Combine the whipping cream, sweetened condensed milk, coffee, and vanilla. Chill.

Beat with an electric mixer on low speed until slightly thickened. Fold in the crushed toffee. Spoon into a 2-quart square baking dish or a 9x5x3-inch loaf pan. Cover and freeze ice cream several hours or until firm. Makes 12 servings.

Nutrition information per serving: 315 calories, 4 g protein, 27 g carbohydrate, 21 g fat (12 g saturated), 68 mg cholesterol, 94 mg sodium.

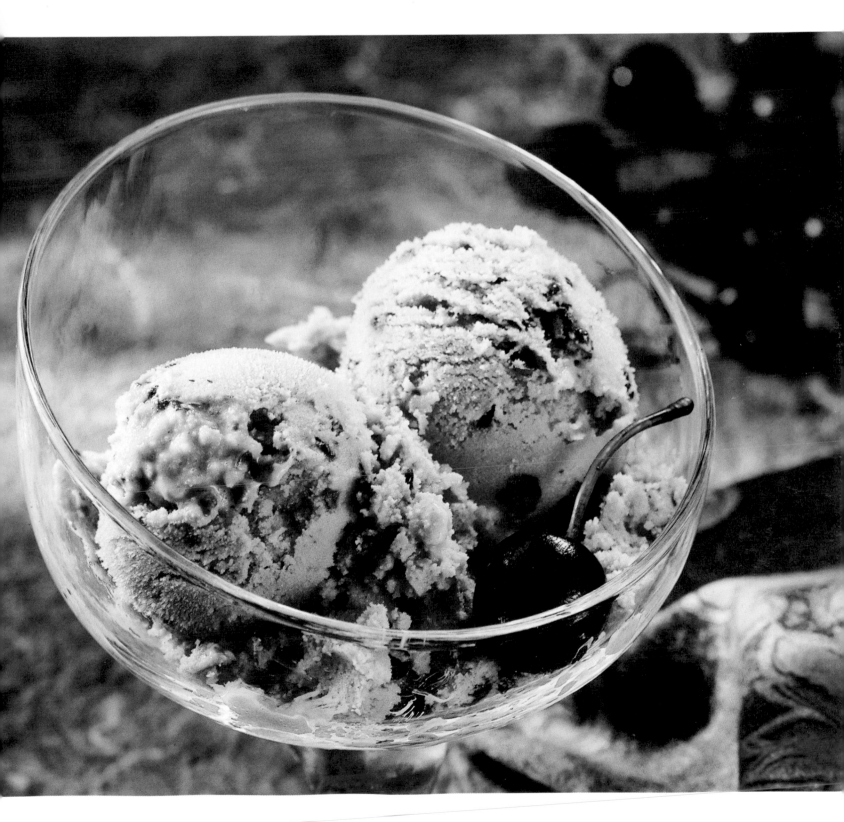

Frosty Chocolate-Cherry Yogurt

CONTENTS

METRIC COOKING HINTS

By making a few conversions, cooks in Australia, Canada, and the United Kingdom can use the recipes in this book with confidence. The charts on this page provide a guide for converting measurements from the U.S. customary system, which is used throughout this book, to the imperial and metric systems. There also is a conversion table for oven temperatures to accommodate the differences in oven calibrations.

Product Differences: Most of the ingredients called for in the recipes in this book are available in English-speaking countries. However, some are known by different names. Here are some common U.S. American ingredients and their possible counterparts:

• Sugar is granulated or castor sugar.
• Powdered sugar is icing sugar.
• All-purpose flour is plain household flour or white flour. When self-rising flour is used in place of all-purpose flour in a recipe that calls for leavening, omit the leavening agent (baking soda or baking powder) and salt.
• Light-colored corn syrup is golden syrup.
• Cornstarch is cornflour.
• Baking soda is bicarbonate of soda.
• Vanilla is vanilla essence.
• Green, red, or yellow sweet peppers are capsicums.
• Golden raisins are sultanas.

Volume and Weight: U.S. Americans traditionally use cup measures for liquid and solid ingredients. The chart, above right, shows the approximate imperial and metric equivalents. If you are accustomed to weighing solid ingredients, the following approximate equivalents will help.

• 1 cup butter, castor sugar, or rice = 8 ounces = about 230 grams
• 1 cup flour = 4 ounces = about 115 grams
• 1 cup icing sugar = 5 ounces = about 140 grams

Spoon measures are used for smaller amounts of ingredients. Although the size of the tablespoon varies slightly in different countries, for practical purposes and for recipes in this book, a straight substitution is all that's necessary.

Measurements made using cups or spoons always should be level unless stated otherwise.

Metric Information
EQUIVALENTS: U.S. = AUSTRALIA/U.K.

⅛ teaspoon = 1 ml	½ cup = 120 ml
¼ teaspoon = 1.25 ml	⅔ cup = 160 ml
½ teaspoon = 2.5 ml	¾ cup = 180 ml
1 teaspoon = 5 ml	1 cup = 240 ml
1 tablespoon = 15 ml	2 cups = 475 ml
1 fluid ounce = 30 ml	1 quart = 1 liter
¼ cup = 60 ml	½ inch = 1.25 cm
⅓ cup = 80 ml	1 inch = 2.5 cm

BAKING PAN SIZES

U.S. American	Metric
8x1½-inch round baking pan	20x4-cm cake tin
9x1½-inch round baking pan	23x4-cm cake tin
11x7x1½-inch baking pan	28x18x4-cm baking tin
13x9x2-inch baking pan	32x23x5-cm baking tin
2-quart rectangular baking dish	28x18x4-cm baking tin
15x10x1-inch baking pan	38x25.5x2.5-cm baking tin (Swiss roll tin)
9-inch pie plate	22x4- or 23x4-cm pie plate
7- or 8-inch springform pan	18- or 20-cm springform or loose-bottom cake tin
9x5x3-inch loaf pan	23x13x8-cm or 2-pound narrow loaf tin or pâté tin
1½-quart casserole	1.5-liter casserole
2-quart casserole	2-liter casserole

OVEN TEMPERATURE EQUIVALENTS

Fahrenheit Setting	Celsius Setting*	Gas Setting
300°F	150°C	Gas mark 2 (very low)
325°F	170°C	Gas mark 3 (low)
350°F	180°C	Gas mark 4 (moderate)
375°F	190°C	Gas mark 5 (moderately hot)
400°F	200°C	Gas mark 6 (hot)
425°F	220°C	Gas mark 7 (hot)
450°F	230°C	Gas mark 8 (very hot)
475°F	240°C	Gas mark 9 (very hot)
Broil		Grill

*Electric and gas ovens may be calibrated using Celsius. However, for an electric oven, increase the Celsius setting 10 to 20 degrees when cooking above 160°C. For convection or forced-air ovens (gas or electric), lower the temperature setting 10°C when cooking at all heat levels.